'Fourteen years ago, Elizabeth West and her husband, Alan, left Bristol for Hafod, some sixteen miles south of Colwyn Bay. In a cottage with its run-down buildings they made their home. *Garden in the Hills* is the tale of a struggle to wrench a livelihood from a windswept patch of scrubby hillside where the line of demarcation between the desert and the sown was always vague and there was little time for the book of verses to vary the hard grind.

'The author's delight in birds, animals, insects, wild flowers and trees is infectious ... Elizabeth West talked to them all, holding that anything that has life will respond to love. And out of this love grew her concern for the future of wild nature.

'In the underlying urgency of the book, readers will, hopefully, become more aware of the threat to our environment now that the bulldozer is fast becoming the solution of many a rural problem.'
Irish Press

Also by Elizabeth West

HOVEL IN THE HILLS
KITCHEN IN THE HILLS
SUFFER LITTLE CHILDREN
and published by Corgi Books

Elizabeth West

Garden in the Hills

CORGI BOOKS

GARDEN IN THE HILLS
A CORGI BOOK 0 552 11707 2

Originally published in Great Britain by
Faber & Faber Ltd.

PRINTING HISTORY
Faber & Faber edition published 1980
Corgi edition published 1981
Corgi edition reprinted 1982
Corgi edition reprinted 1985
Corgi edition reprinted 1987

Corgi Books are published by Transworld Publishers
Ltd., 61–63 Uxbridge Road, Ealing, London W5 5SA, in
Australia by Transworld Publishers (Aust.) Pty. Ltd.,
15–23 Helles Avenue, Moorebank, NSW 2170, and in New
Zealand by Transworld Publishers (N.Z.) Ltd., Cnr. Moselle
and Waipareira Avenues, Henderson, Auckland.

Printed and bound in Great Britain by
Cox & Wyman Ltd., Reading, Berks.

Contents

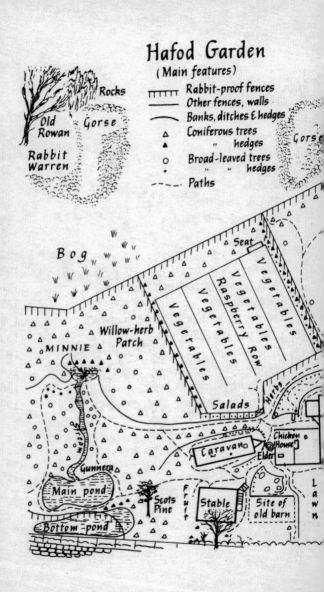

Hafod Garden
(Main features)

⊥⊥⊥⊥	Rabbit-proof fences
────	Other fences, walls
⌒⌒⌒	Banks, ditches & hedges
△	Coniferous trees
▲	" hedges
○	Broad-leaved trees
•	" " hedges
– – –	Paths

Rocks

Old Rowan Gorse

Rabbit Warren

Gorse

Bog

Seat

Vegetables

Raspberry Row

Vegetables

Vegetables

Vegetables

Willow-herb Patch

MINNIE

Salads

Herbs

Caravan

Chicken House

Elder

Gunnera

Site of old barn

Main pond

Scots Pine

Fruit

Stable

Lawn

Bottom-pond

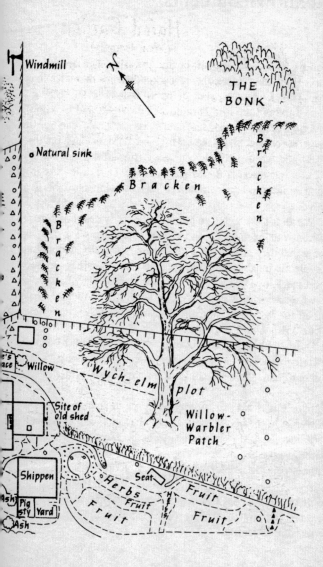

Windmill

N

THE
BONK

o Natural sink

Bracken

Bracken

Bracken

Bracken

Willow

Wych-elm plot

Site of
old shed

Willow-
Warbler
Patch

Shippen

Seat

Herbs

Fruit

Ash

Pig
sty Yard

Fruit

Fruit

Fruit

Ash

Acknowledgments

You have to climb the hill behind the cottage in order to see our neighbours. Over there, on the left, is Mr. Thomas's farm—his land is in front of ours, and those sturdy Welsh Black bullocks are his. Turn now to the right, and look in the direction of the Carneddau land mass, and you can see the farm owned by Mr. Jones. His land borders ours on three sides, and we usually buy our eggs from him. Look straight ahead now, towards the Migneint Hills. That little cluster of stone buildings in the middle distance is the farm of Evan Lloyd.

We don't see a lot of our neighbours; weeks may go by without our exchanging more than a passing wave, but we know that they are always *there*—quietly friendly, helpful and completely reliable. Of all our neighbours it is perhaps to Beryl and Evan Lloyd that we owe the most thanks. They have given us wise advice as well as practical help. It is to them we have turned for assistance on many occasions, and they have never let us down.

Our neighbours have provided the 'background' to our life at Hafod. They do not appear very much in this book . . . but, without them, the book could never have been written.

Perhaps this is also an appropriate place to acknowledge Dic, Dilwen, Gwen and Muriel. These characters are completely fictitious. They do not exist anywhere, except in my imagination. I invented them so that I could describe true incidents without causing embarrassment to real people.

Some of the material in Chapter 4 has appeared in *The Countryman*, and my thanks are due to the Editor for his kind permission to reprint.

GARDEN IN THE HILLS

1. Us

'The trouble with you,' said Alan, 'is that you just don't concentrate.'

I eased my aching insteps one at a time from the rung of the ladder, and reflected upon his remark. Last night's snowstorm had now abated and we were mending the shippen roof. Leastways, *Alan* was mending the roof, *I* was standing on top of a ladder and holding the end of another ladder which lay up the slope of the roof and supported him and his tools, a pile of slates and some wire netting. My arms, stretched upwards and clasping the sides of his ladder, were numb with the cold. A bitter wind laced with snow and occasional hailstones lashed at my exposed wrists and face. Occasional gobbets of icy snow and bits of broken slate hurtled down the roof and straight into my gaping coat sleeves. I was shivering, aching and bad-tempered. I couldn't see what concentration had to do with it. 'If you'd fixed the damned roof in the summer we wouldn't be spending Christmas Day doing this!' I snarled back.

It was an unfair retort. I knew perfectly well that during fine summer days there were other things to do—like repointing the chimney-stack, lime-washing the south-west-facing front of the cottage, repainting doors and window frames, repairing fences, cutting thistles and earning a living. It wasn't as though the shippen was needed to shelter cows. It contained stacks of timber, fencing wire, slates, useful junk and a quantity of packing cases whose contents have been but partially investigated since we moved here from Bristol thirteen years ago. The only livestock using the shippen these days are a roosting blackbird, an occasional nesting wren and a colony of field-mice who make cosy nests each year in a packing case of old *Tatler* magazines. There is little danger of a population explosion amongst our township of field-mice, because during the winter months a polecat moves in from the moors and makes short work of the *Tatler*ville residents. This nicely balanced community of wild-life is welcome to the facilities of our shippen, but has to be content with premises that are but roughly patched up as and when necessary.

Summers are short here in North Wales, and on this high moorland the weather can be treacherous—weeks of wind and rain alternating with long drought-stricken periods of shimmering heat. Fine, balmy days are so precious they present a dilemma. Do we just sit around and enjoy them? Or do we tackle some of the jobs that have to be done? We linger over breakfast, wandering along to the spring clutching a cup of coffee and a piece of toast. We discuss the jobs that could be done. The grass needs hacking back around the vegetable plot; on the other hand, it might be too hot for that, and the flies could be a nuisance. How about sorting through an out-building? On a fine day like this when you can actually *see* inside the old stone buildings we could have a real turn-out. But isn't it rather a pity to work indoors? We sit beside the spring whilst we discuss the problem further. Should we perhaps put a coat of bitumen on the stable roof? Alan settles back into his stone seat as he considers this idea. The saxifrage on the bank behind him nestles around his shoulders, and a bee is fussing amongst the flowers. 'I think it's going to be too hot. No good putting on bitumen in really hot weather.' My seat is a slab of sandstone. It is already warmed by the sun and feels luxurious to my thighs. 'A good day for washing,' I muse, 'perhaps I should do the blankets.' A chaffinch comes to bathe in a shallow pool. She splashes flappily, sending sprays of droplets all around her. A dragon-fly darts across the water and hovers with its nose almost touching the bank. The sun is warm on the back of my neck, and a lark soars upwards from the hillside behind us. I notice that our cups are empty. 'I think I'll get some more coffee. This is obviously going to need a lot of discussion. . . .'

We live 'out of step' with the rest of society. To most people their means of earning a living is of first importance; where to live is a secondary consideration. *We* found a humble and isolated smallholding and decided to live there. We then set about thinking how to make a living. Readers of my previous book, *Hovel in the Hills*, will remember that the problem of making money was never satisfactorily solved, and they may be surprised to learn that we are still battling with it. This probably suggests that we are a pair of life's failures. On the other hand, we have somehow managed to survive on a wind-swept patch of scrubby hillside that we chose to call home. How do you measure failure? We are certainly very poor. But we don't need very much money to live here, and as we don't want to live anywhere else our poverty is not at all painful. For us, North Wales means a few acres of moorland in Hiraethog with a backcloth of mountain ranges and a great open sky. We have never been up Snowdon, nor down a slate mine, nor on a narrow-gauge railway, nor visited the coastal resorts (with the exception of trips to a dentist in Colwyn Bay and a car-parts retailer in Rhyl). We sometimes potter around the lanes on our bicycles and occasionally spend a day walking in the hills. But, from choice, we never go very far nor for very long. Time spent away from home somehow feels like wasted time.

For one thing, there is so much to do. And if you have not read about our way of life before, I feel that some explanation is called for. (Readers of *Hovel in the Hills* may skip the rest of this chapter!)

We have a stone and slate cottage and a range of outbuild-ings, all of which need some sort of attention most of the time. Our holding, known as Hafod, consists of a shippen, stable, outhouse, lean-to chicken house and a pigsty. These buildings contain our bicycles, a large assortment of tools, 'interesting' ironmongery, garden implements, and box after box of useful junk. We also have two privies, one of which now contains the mangle. The cottage has five rooms and is just about big enough to contain the two of us, our domestic possessions—and quite a lot of useful junk.

In case you are wondering about all that 'useful junk', let me explain that when one lives in isolation upon a remote moorland far away from any builders' merchants or handyman stores (which one couldn't afford to patronize anyway), one needs to possess a large selection of timber, ironmongery, building materials and tools in order to give attention to slates that fall off, walls that fall out and roofs that are in danger of falling in. When one is also making one's own electricity, repairing one's own shoes, clothes, furniture and machinery, you can see that there is no end to the number of cardboard and wooden boxes that can be filled with 'things that might come in useful'.

Nothing is wasted. Nothing is thrown away if there is the remotest possibility that it might have another use. In this way we have held ourselves and the place together for the past thirteen years. Our methods are usually unorthodox—but they work. Alan now feels that, provided he can lay his hands on a suitable tool and some appropriate material, he can tackle any job that crops up. Take that hole in the shippen roof, for example. You are possibly wondering what on earth he was doing up on the roof with wire netting. (If you saw the state of the rafters you would wonder what on earth he was doing on the roof at all!) Well, he was using wire netting because that was the most appropriate material to use in the circumstances; the circumstances being that the temperature was well below freezing—(no good using cement)—the roof was snow-covered—(no good using glazing tape)—and there was no question of re-nailing the slates to the battens because nearly all the slates were broken when they fell and the 'battens' were merely rotten and broken laths measuring only $\frac{7}{10}$ in $\times \frac{3}{20}$ in in section. So what did Alan do? He roughly renewed the battens using bits of wood previously split for kindling (nailed gently into parts of the rafters that were not too rotten to hold) and fixed the broken slates with tingles* made of $\frac{1}{2}$-inch wire netting, which is easy to cut and manipulate in below-freezing conditions. And, in case you know something about roof repairs and are boggling now at the reference to cement and

* Elongated S-shaped clips, usually made of lead, for fixing loose slates without having to strip the whole roof.

glazing tape, let me assure you that for roofs in the condition of ours, these materials are quite satisfactory. Two-inch glazing tape will secure a slate quite firmly to its neighbour, provided it is pressed down firmly on all sides. We have one roof where every slate is secured in this way, and for twelve years it has needed no attention except for one coat of bitumen to preserve the tape. Previously, every slate on the roof was loose and rattled crazily in the wind; now they lie firm, secure and weathertight.

Cementing a slate back into position is a rougher sort of job, and it is not a good idea to go all over the roof using this method unless the roof timbers are good enough to stand the extra weight. (We don't think ours are.) But cement is cheaper than glazing tape so we use it quite often when repairing roofs on outbuildings.

All in all, I seem to spend a lot of time standing on a ladder hanging on to the end of another ladder which is lying on a roof. I am frequently bad-tempered on these occasions because I am so uneasy. I don't like to see Alan on a roof on any occasion, and when he's up there with a weighty bucket of cement I jibber with anxiety. Is the whole roof about to collapse inwards, perhaps, with Alan disappearing in a noisy cloud of broken slates, dry rot and woodworm? Or will the ladder suddenly slew sideways and catapult him and his bucket off the gable-end? I hang on grimly, fearing the worst. And then there is the problem of falling dollops of cement. Anything Alan drops will come straight down to me. It is pointless looking up to see what is coming because no evasive action can be taken. If I am wearing a thick hat and a boilersuit buttoned at neck and cuffs, then it doesn't matter very much. But I must be prepared to suffer if the weather is hot and I am wearing a blouse with gaping sleeves and an open neck. Sloshy great lumps come hurtling down the roof. I stand there stoically whilst my brassière fills with cement.

We work together on most jobs; he the 'master-craftsman', I the labouring-mate. There is nothing in this relationship for Women's Lib to get upset about. It is a perfectly sensible work-

ing partnership; each giving according to ability. Where practical matters are concerned, my ability is nil. I am the sort of
idiot who has to have taps labelled 'turn off this way', with an
arrow pointing. What's more, I have to read this instruction
each time I use the tap. If something I am using fails to operate, *my*
only remedy is to hit or shake it. If I want something that goes
wrong fixed I know there is really only one course of action.
Fetch Alan.

I once mended a puncture. Cycling home from Llanrwst one
day, I ran over a hawthorn twig and within a couple of minutes
my back tyre was flat. I sat beside the road and considered the
matter. The piece of hawthorn was still sticking to the tyre, so
it was obvious where the puncture was. If I wheeled my machine home for the remaining four miles (with a saddlebag
heavy with shopping), I might ruin the tyre and damage the
rim. This was a quiet country lane and there was no chance of
a lift. I had a complete puncture repair outfit in the saddlebag
pocket. It was a fine evening and I had plenty of time. I could
think of no excuse for not having a go at mending this puncture.
I removed the saddlebag, up-ended the bike, took out the
repair outfit and started to prise off the tyre as I had seen Alan
do so many times. I won't bore you with the details of the
entire performance. Sufficient to say that some twenty minutes
later I stood proudly, and with filthy hands, surveying a back
tyre which was now hard and ready to be ridden again. When
I arrived home, late but triumphant, Alan was incredulous—
and suspicious. 'I think I had better have a look,' he said,
wheeling the bike out of the outhouse again. Once more the
machine was turned upside down and Alan examined the back
wheel. 'I thought you said you mended it?' he said, pressing
his thumb into the rapidly softening tyre, 'And did you *have* to
pinch the inner tube like that?' He pointed to an elongated
bubble at the side of the rim. That wasn't all either. I had put
so much rubber solution on the patch it had squeezed out all
around it and had stuck that whole area of tube to the inside of
the tyre; moreover, I had forgotten to remove the offending
thorn, which accounted for the fact that another puncture was

already visible in the repair patch. To crown it all, I had lost the tyre levers. Is it any wonder that Alan considers a shovel or a pickaxe to be the only sort of tool I can safely be allowed to handle, and is generally happier if I stick to fetching, carrying and taking orders?

As a matter of fact, fetching and carrying is something I don't mind doing; which is just as well because we have no mains services at Hafod. This means quite a lot of to-ing and fro-ing with buckets . . . *in* with the water, *out* with the vegetable peelings, *in* with the coal and logs, *out* with the ashes. I trudge around quite happily, working to a routine that is leisurely in summer, but sometimes a bit hasty in wintertime when all the outside chores must be done before darkness falls. But it is no hardship to live like this. You may be appalled that we don't have any plumbing, but we don't have any plumbing problems either—like leaking radiators, frozen pipes, overflowing cisterns. And what about that water tank up in your roof? When did you last have a look at it? How do you know it is not almost rusted through and about to cascade water through the bed-room ceiling? How often do you have your central heating system overhauled? We don't have worries like these. We just go to the spring and fetch a bucket of water. Bath night? We use a galvanized tub in the kitchen in front of the stove or, in warm weather, a watering can at the spring.

Stove is the most important thing in our cottage. Stove is fed with coal, twigs, logs and rubbish and in return cooks the dinner, heats the water and warms the cottage. Stove is alight day and night all year round, only to be let out for an annual overhaul and chimney sweep, or when we have to leave the cottage for two days or more. Stove has a long hotplate, two ovens and a 16-gallon hot-water tank. We could, presumably, manage without Stove. We have an open fireplace in the parlour with a pair of trivets to take kettles and saucepans. We also have a selection of Primus paraffin cookers. But managing without Stove would be hardship. That would mean getting up to a cold house and having to light the fire before tea could be brewed. Stove gives us luxury and comfort all the time. We can

manage quite well without plumbing, but we wouldn't like to
be without Stove.

Caring for Stove (which involves uncomplicated things like
stoking up with coal, riddling out the ashes and scraping the
flues clean of soot) is my responsibility. Providing electricity is
Alan's.

It wasn't that we desperately needed electricity. It was just
that Alan was intrigued with the idea of making it. We are
1,000 feet above sea-level and exposed to wind from all quarters, and he could see no reason why the ill wind that tore off
our slates shouldn't be put to some good by turning a windmill.
So we acquired an elderly Lucas Freelite windcharger which
supplies us with electricity, provided that:

    (a) the wind is blowing hard enough to turn the blades, or
    (b) the wind is not blowing so hard that it has to be furled,
        and
    (c) regular and frequent maintenance is carried out.

With regard to (c), I find that, as electrician's mate, I am
once again standing upon a ladder. This time at the bottom,
whilst Alan at the top ministers to the needs of a dynamo, pro-
pellor and tail vane atop a 13-foot post. This sort of ladder job is
not so bad. I don't feel that Alan is in much danger and, anyway, I am completely captivated by the view up here on the
hillside behind the house. A vast landscape of moorland and
mountain lies all around us. I can see the farmhouses and
buildings of three neighbours—neat little grey clusters huddling
in the soft folds of the moor. And the air is thin and clear. I
take great gulping breaths of it and gaze around in wonderment
at the sunlight and shadow racing across the hills—until I'm
asked what the hell I'm wriggling about for and if I don't
watch out I will have him off in a minute.

On the occasions when we are unable to have electricity we
use paraffin lamps, and we are quite happy to accept their
limitations. Paraffin lamps have a soft, romantic glow. They
also have a distinct smell and nasty habits. Turn your back on
them, and they will go up in flames and smoke. Forget to fill
them, and you will be hastily groping for candles just when the

radio play you are listening to has reached its exciting climax. But, having got used to their nasty habits, we still think they have a soft, romantic glow, and when we are away from home a whiff of paraffin will set us thinking soft, romantic thoughts. But we don't rely upon paraffin any more than we do upon electricity. We also have candles, acetylene lamps and electric torches. Electric torches are essential for Going Outside After Dark. A candle is apt to blow out—probably just when you have fumbled for and dropped the toilet roll.

This brings me to another aspect of our lives that horrifies some people. The privy. Admittedly it is a little chilly out there in wintertime, and one certainly doesn't hang about any longer than is necessary, but does that really matter very much? Of course, someone has to empty the bucket, but we are not squeamish about this. It has simply become another chore that has to be done, usually once a week, and usually by Alan.

All these chores take time. There are only the two of us, yet we seem to spend a large part of each day just coping with the day-to-day requirements of living. But we feel a tremendous satisfaction in being independent of The System. Moreover we are *here*, where we want to be, so who minds a few humble chores?

There are times, however, when we are not here, when we have to go away in order to earn some money. And when I am away from Hafod, pulling a flush on someone else's lavatory cistern, or turning a tap at someone else's sink, I think longingly of home. Who wants tap-water? *I* don't. I am happy with my bucket at the spring. Neither do I want to walk up someone else's carpeted stairs to the bathroom. I would much rather be at home, clutching my electric torch and nipping out the back into the dark, frosty night.

Going away from home occasionally in order to earn money is something we have ruefully come to accept because we have found no continuously successful way of earning a living here. We came with nothing to offer the local community but en-thusiasm and a willingness to tackle anything. City bred and working class (I was an office worker, Alan repaired office machinery), we had no skills of any use to hill farmers, no profession, no 'background' and no useful contacts. We found the local employment exchange full of unemployed Welshmen and empty of jobs. It was hardly surprising that we were unwelcome. So we found casual jobs for ourselves, and have hopped from one job to another ever since; sometimes local, sometimes not so local, but always temporary and always insecure. But we bought this patch of land and stout little cottage without going into debt, so it doesn't seem to matter very much that our earnings are low and irregular.

We came to North Wales because we wanted solitude, and to breathe air that was clean. Also—in a world of shifting insecurity and impending chaos—we wanted to live in a landscape that had not changed much over the centuries. We found this at Hafod. Our nearest neighbour is a mile or so away, and the wind across the heath has a scent to it that has something to do with wild gorse, bracken, damp peat and lichen covered stones. Our mountains are timeless. This wilderness was here when the Romans marched up the Conwy valley, and when the Normans built Caernarfon Castle. We hope it will last our lifetime.

The other day, whilst rummaging through a box of stuff-we-will-give-to-a-jumble-sale-if-anyone-ever-calls-for-it, I came across one of those little dollies with a large, crocheted crinoline skirt that people who like that sort of thing place over their toilet rolls. This had been given to us many years ago by a well-meaning friend . . . 'for you to put in your bathroom, when you eventually have one.' It was, of course, assumed by friends and neighbours that we had bought our cottage to 'do up', and that after an initial light-hearted period of putting up with primitive conditions, we would set about doing all the decent, civilized things like having mains water and electricity laid on, building a bathroom, and acquiring all the necessities of life like a telephone, refrigerator. washing machine, vacuum cleaner and television set. In fact we want none of these things. We have made our cottage weathertight and draught-proof; we have made it warm and cosy (to our standards) and we have organized a domestic routine that copes with the chores satisfactorily. We do not wish to change anything. A lot of people who talk about 'getting away from it all' really want to 'take it all with them'. We have never felt that urge. We gratefully accept what Hafod has to give us. We ask for nothing more.

In the meantime thirteen years have passed, and we are now middle-aged. What have we achieved? We own a primitive cottage and a few acres of rough grazing. But we have no regular employment.

What have we done with our lives?

We have made a garden.

2. In the beginning

Neither Alan nor I were particularly interested in gardening until we married. In my childhood home Dad was the gardener, with Mum leaning over his shoulder telling him what to do. So far as I was concerned the garden was somewhere to sunbathe, although I could occasionally be called upon to do something like dig a bean trench or mow the lawn (my penchant for manual labour having established itself at an early age).

In Alan's household his mother did the gardening. I gather that neither Alan nor his father ever lifted a spade or a pair of shears. The garden was a useful place in which to take a bicycle to pieces, or sit and read the evening paper.

As soon as we married we became interested in growing things. Our first attempts at vegetable cultivation were carried out in an 8-foot-square plot in the rear lawn of the garden of our first town flat. We were allowed to use this patch (which we shared with a fifty-two-year-old rose tree) in return for taking on the chore of keeping the whole garden tidy. We grew cottagers' kale, turnips, onions, lettuces, radishes, beetroot, parsley and thyme. We even managed, by surreptitious nibbling with the spade at the edge of the plot, to increase its size to about 9 foot square; which was quite an achievement, considering that all our gardening efforts were constantly supervised by the landlord peering out from his first-floor flat. He cramped our style in other respects too. He was very friendly with his next-door neighbour, whose three cats used our plot as their lavatory. He took a very dim view of our stone-throwing, and told us so. We also suspect that it was he who stole our lettuces from time to time. On the whole it's surprising that our enthusiasm for gardening grew.

Our second town flat allowed us the free use of a 20-foot-square paved courtyard which contained a 3-foot-wide flower border on three sides. The garden was walled; a perfect sun trap. Against the back wall, and in between the hyacinths, primulas, irises, aubretia and roses, we grew tomatoes. By ruthlessly cutting back the aubretia we gained space enough for a few seed-beds and we sowed lettuces, radishes, parsley and carrots, but once again we were plagued by visiting cats. Here we were able to throw stones uninterrupted, but we were fighting a losing battle. There were just too many cats, too often. (The half pound of pepper we scattered around had no deterrent effect whatsoever.) The ground became so fouled that we didn't like putting our hands into it, and we became squeamish about eating root crops from it. In the end we settled for tomatoes, tomatoes and more tomatoes.

I suppose that the only sure way of keeping cats away from your garden is to keep a dog. But there is possibly another way: keep a cat—a large, aggressive male who has not been robbed of his manhood. According to my observations, cats *never* relieve themselves in their own gardens. So if your cat is a pugnacious male, he will do his dirty work in your neighbour's seed-bed, whilst guarding your plot from other feline marauders. A sure way of disposing of your cat problem and acquiring a neighbour problem. Take your choice.

At Hafod we have no such problems. The only cats we ever glimpse are families of feral ones (domestic cats 'gone wild' several generations back) who come to take up temporary residence in the bracken or amongst the odds and ends in the ruined pigsty. We don't like them, but we don't usually discover them until it's too late—when we find ourselves confronted by a scrawny, scabby mother cat, hissing defiance over her scruffy little brood. We leave them alone. They are vagrants and will sooner or later take themselves off. In the meantime we hope that they will sort out our vole and mouse population a bit.

We notice that these feline tramps scorn the prim toilet habits of their tame cousins. None of this digging a little hole and scratching earth over the contents. They just drop their deposit wherever they happen to be—on the grass, earth or path—and then walk away from it with never a backward glance. Deplorable manners maybe, but definitely easier for the gardener to cope with.

The experience we gained when gardening in town didn't really help us much at Hafod, because we soon learned that the main problem here is weather. Welsh moorland weather *can* mean hushed, dewy mornings; airy, sunlit afternoons and tranquil, majestic evenings. When we get visitors under these conditions they wonder what we're fussing about. They look in amazement at the boulders weighting down the corrugated iron on the chicken house roof, and they raise their eyebrows at our standard may tree lashed with leather straps to its wrought iron stake. They stumble into the 15-inch-deep stormwater trench that surrounds the vegetable plot and wonder what on earth it's for. But they don't come when the weather is bad. Any prudent motorist turns back when he finds his wipers being blown off the windscreen in a moorland gale. And there's something about the sight of a mountain stream about to burst its banks that causes an intending visitor to remember urgent business elsewhere.

It is the *extreme* nature of the weather that is so bothersome. A brilliant sun can glare down at us from a hard blue sky for several weeks at a time, and we pad around in bare feet and sun hats, praying for rain. The soil in the vegetable garden turns to buff-coloured dust and small stones. Long cracks appear in the lawn. Then comes the rain; and having come, it stays. Day after day after day. Then, when the moorland above us has soaked up its fill, the water comes rolling down the hillside to Hafod. Every gully becomes a small stream; every mole hole a water spout. With the rain comes the wind, battering the house and wrenching at the trees. The peas and beans are smashed to the ground; the artichokes are broken off at crazy angles. We blunder about the sodden foliage in sou'westers and wellington boots, working desperately with pickaxe and shovel to keep the drainage channels free so that most of the water may pass by us, and not through us.

People who have lived on this moorland all their lives accept its moods placidly. So the flood water burst up through the floor of the kitchen. So what? They just shrug their shoulders and sweep it out again. So the gale blew away the chicken house and fourteen bantams are dead. So what? They just shrug their shoulders and buy some more next market day. So today is scorching hot, and tomorrow it's throwing down hailstones. So what? It's worthy of comment to your neighbour certainly, but that's all—it doesn't mean that you have to dress differently. I have never seen a hill farmer take off his coat in the sun, nor don a raincoat in wet weather. We once gave a pair of fleecy-lined PVC gauntlet gloves to our friend Dic who lives the other side of the moor. These gloves had been given to Alan by a well-meaning friend, but they were much too tight for either of us, so we handed them on to Dic. He is a small man, and we had often seen him driving his tractor, hunched up against the rain, with his bony, red hands clutching the wheel. He was delighted with his gift. He held the gloves reverently between finger and thumb, then searched his tractor for a clean cranny in which to put them. He carried them home and placed them in a drawer in the Welsh dresser alongside a Fairisle pullover that his sister had knitted him. He occasionally showed them to us when we visited. 'Still got those gloves. See?' So far as we know, neither gloves nor pullover were ever worn.

I first met Dic when I was out inspecting our boundary fences just after we had moved in. It had been raining and blowing hard for three days, but that morning the snarling southwester had veered to become a blasting northwester, a change of direction which I hadn't noticed as I stepped out of the front door. I was all braced up to meet the wind straight in my face, only to be knocked sideways by a blast in the ear. As I was walking alongside the hedge that separates us from the road, Dic suddenly appeared in a gap between two boughs of hawthorn; a very damp but grinning little man in a shapeless cloth jacket. With water streaming down his face he wished me a polite 'Good morning'. I returned his greeting, and we just stood there beaming at each other—he obviously curious to find out what these strangers at Hafod were like, and me obviously anxious to prove that we were harmless. In true British fashion we bridged the awkwardness between us by discussing the weather. 'Does the wind often blow from this direction?' I yelled. He shook his head and pointed to the south-west. 'It will die down this evening,' he shouted. 'Tomorrow it will be cloudy. Not much rain.' I was impressed. A lifetime on the moors had given this man some instinctive knowledge of weather patterns that was beyond my comprehension. He belonged to this wilderness. He was as much a part of it as the twisted hawthorns, the tumbling rocks and the rolling seas of bracken. Which of his senses perceived a change in the weather? Was it something he saw in the shape of the clouds racing across the sky from the Carneddau? Or was it just a certain 'feeling' in the wind. 'How do you know?' I asked. His reply was torn out of his mouth in another northwesterly gust '. . . on the telly,' he said.

The piece of land we own is odd-shaped and uneven. Vaguely squarish with an adjoining quadrangle at the southern corner, it slopes from about 980 to 1,050 feet above sea-level. The cottage, with its huddle of outbuildings, squats near the bottom of the slope. The spring lies about thirty yards from the back door (more or less on the same level as the cottage) and the first job we did was to put up a fence so that the spring was included in the area of land we intended to make into a garden. Our field is now a steeply sloping square of bracken, rock and gorse, with the southern corner fenced off. Our garden is all the other bits—amounting to about two-thirds of an acre.

The piece of land between the front door and the road was divided by a drive which ran straight down to the gate (a distance of about forty yards). To the left of the drive was an oblong plateau containing long, rank grass (since identified as Yorkshire fog) and a graceful wych-elm. To the right of the drive was a sunken, triangular hollow. The plateau was prevented from sliding down on to the drive by a bulging retaining wall, topped by a hawthorn hedge. Another hawthorn hedge screened our land from the road, and it was the sunken hollow between the hedges—filled with nettles, docks, hogweeds, bits of corrugated iron, barbed wire, tin cans, bottles, cinders and a broken motor cycle side-car—that we called the front garden.

Alan could see great possibilities. He visualized neat, walled terraces, connecting grassy paths and curved flights of stone steps. I was unable to share his vision. I just saw corrugated iron, barbed wire, tin cans, bottles, cinders and a motor cycle side-car and wondered where on earth we'd begin.

It is said that a glance at a front garden will tell you something about the occupants of the house. To a certain extent this is true. Those who wish to conform can be picked out quite easily from the non-conformists, the show-offs, the don't-cares and the can't-copes. Everyone's front garden *says* something. So did the front garden at Hafod. It said 'No one has wanted or cared for me for a long time. Please help me.' So we did.

Removing rubbish was the first job.

The trouble with removing rubbish when you have plenty of space is that you find yourself *continually* removing it because the place you dumped it yesterday is exactly the spot where you want to plant something today. Move it again, and you will find, tomorrow, that you have chosen the only place that is just right for stacking some newly cut logs, or dumping a load of coal. I am referring now to the 'might-come-in-useful' rubbish such as sheets of corrugated iron, fencing wire, pieces of timber and old slates. (I dug a hole and buried the bottles, cans and—believe it or not—the motor cycle side-car.)

Sifting through other people's rubbish can be quite an absorbing task, especially as you work your way back through the broken radio and plastic bucket era to an earlier age of leather harness, brass buckles and hand-thrown stoneware bottles. Why is it that a grimy, aluminium pressure cooker (1950 vintage) is slightly distasteful, yet a rusting iron cooking pot (1880 vintage) is 'interesting'? One day we came across some parts of a horse-powered gin which had once been used to drive a butter churn in the back kitchen. These machines were once fairly common and were used on isolated farmsteads for such purposes as butter churning, chaff cutting and corn grinding.

There were a few water-wheels in this district too. They were used mainly to drive *pandai* (tucking or fulling mills). Most of these have now been destroyed, some quite recently. They have gone the way of Hafod horse gin: cut up and sold for their scrap-iron value. All that was left of our machine was about eighteen feet of drive-shaft which was buried four feet deep under rubble and old slates, and this was coupled to the rem-nant of another shaft by a very modern-looking universal joint. All the other parts above ground and in the house were gone. In the back kitchen wall we found the place where the shaft had originally gone through. It had been very roughly filled in. Alan made a little 'keep hole' there—just to preserve an interesting feature of earlier days at Hafod.

As Alan was the one with the visions and the plans, he directed the operations and, once again, I was the taker of orders. The removal of rubbish was the first order, of course; then came the clearing of undergrowth. I have now become very skilled at this particular task and can give advice on the subject to anyone who wants it. First of all the growth must be cut as close to the ground as possible. This greenery must be removed (to the compost heap of course), then the ground dug with a fork. The first time you attempt to push the fork into the ground you may find you can penetrate only a half inch or so. Shift the fork around a bit and try again. After a few attempts you will find a spot where the prongs of the fork will sink in be-tween the nettle roots, stones, old boots and cans. Push the fork down and then start levering. You will eventually reach a stage where the tip of a fork prong has appeared above the soil level, but the rest of the fork is still submerged beneath the aforementioned nettle roots, stones, cans and old boots. So you now grasp hold of the end of the prong with your left hand, re-taining a hold at the base of the fork handle with your right hand, then you HEAVE and HEAVE, and up it all comes. You then pick yourself up from the undergrowth and go in and put the kettle on for a cup of tea. Alan is somewhat impatient of my method, which takes rather a long time and involves too many cups of tea and too many bent fork prongs, and he will tackle the job with mattock and pickaxe. As I consider that these two tools are liable to cause me some spinal or gynae-cological mischief I give them a wide berth and continue bending fork prongs. Anyway, between the two of us we managed to clear odd patches of ground in the front garden. Before leaving the subject of ground clearance though, I would like to return to the cutting down of the undergrowth at the start of the operation. I found that the best way of doing this was on hands and knees with a pair of garden shears. At first I tried to scythe it. After all—I thought to myself—one was now living in the country, and one must use country tools. Garden shears are for use in suburbia. A friend had given Alan a scythe; now was the time to use it. I had seen men scything grass alongside the roads, and very easy it looked too. Nothing to it. Just swing the scythe in sweeping, graceful curves. Well, to begin with, I found it a very heavy and oddly-balanced implement to use. My first 'graceful curve' travelled about six inches before the scythe point dug into the ground; my second nearly sliced my legs off. It was at this stage that Alan came and took the scythe away from me, and I have never handled it since. I must point out that Alan also finds it awkward to use, even after many adjustments, and he gets on better with a sickle. However, I shall continue crawling about on hands and knees with my garden shears.

This area of land eventually became our herb and fruit garden, but in the early days we concentrated on growing vegetables. In the first patch of cleared ground we sowed cottagers' kale seed, and in the second patch we planted potatoes. Or, to be quite correct, *Alan* sowed seed and planted potatoes. In all the years we have been here I have sown and planted nothing. I don't really understand why, it is just that our work seems to fall into two separate compartments—*his* work and *her* work. For example, *his* work is deciding where the peas shall be sown. *Her* work is digging the trench. *His* work is sorting out the pea canes and netting. *Her* work is filling the trench with compost. *His* work is erecting the canes and netting and sowing the peas and, when they are ready for picking, deciding which pods should be kept for seed and marking them. *Her* work is picking all the other peas and cooking them. At the end of the season *his* work is removing the canes and netting, and throwing them in a heap on the ground. *Her* work is sorting them all out, picking off all the bits of pea vine, folding up the nets and putting them away tidily ready for next year.

I hasten to add that it is only the *humdrum* labouring that is *her* work. Dramatic labouring (like excavating stormwater trenches) or artistic labouring (like shifting boulders to form rockeries) or essential labouring (like pathway engineering) is most definitely *his* work.

The making and laying of pathways around our hummocky, hillocky garden was one of Alan's first jobs. The original paths at Hafod were just mud tracks, which meant that during wet weather we were bringing a lot of mud into the house on our boots. For a while I made a half-hearted attempt to keep the mud at bay by shaking coal cinders around the house; which meant that we were now bringing muddy cinders into the house. Then Alan took over. He ordered a couple of lorry-loads of limestone chippings, also sand and cement. He concreted a small yard outside the back door (about seven square yards) and laid paths of chippings all round the house and down to the gate. This wasn't done in one operation. In fact it was accomplished over several years because Alan takes path-making very seriously. Paths, according to Alan, must always be level, and never be straight. This meant that earth had to be shifted, banks had to be built and steps introduced. The paths must also be drained. There will always be occasions when flood water will swill through the Hafod garden, so all paths had to be drained by gullys at their sides and culverts underneath.

The path to the spring took the longest to sort out. Flood water cuts across it in several places, and we kept changing our minds about the most suitable surface for this path. It is a very important path. I might be staggering along here with my buckets when I am an old woman of eighty. We had to have a surface that would be safe in all weather conditions. The original path was, of course, just a muddy track across the field, with a nasty, slithering, muddy slope for the last few feet to the spring itself. I thought it incredible that for two centuries or more women had been slithering down this muddy slope with their buckets because none of their menfolk had sufficient interest to make the access to the spring any easier for them. My man thought differently. Knowing that a wife with a broken wrist or leg isn't much use, he made a level approach to the spring with paving stones, with a final step down to another paving stone, and incorporated a level ledge upon which to place the bucket. The rest of the path wasn't sorted out so quickly. Should we make it paving stones all the way to the back door, or would it be safer in icy weather to walk on grass? Alan compromised. He laid paving stones one pace apart, which left a grassed space in between each stone wide enough to take a booted foot. The idea was that you could choose—depending upon conditions underfoot—whether to walk upon stone or grass. This was one of those ideas that sound fine in theory, but don't work out in practice. Going to the spring with empty buckets was all right; my pace fell easily upon either stone all the way, or grass all the way—whichever I chose. But coming back with full buckets was a different story. My pace was much shorter and I found myself walking first on stone, then on grass, sometimes half and half. I couldn't walk with a proper rhythm and found it irritating. So the paving stones were prized up, and we thought again. It then occurred to us that the whole idea of laying a surface safe to be walked upon in icy conditions was ridiculous. Under conditions of deep snow it wouldn't make any difference what the under-lying surface was made of, and under freezing rain conditions when the paved surface might be glazed, then one needn't walk upon the path at all. There are other ways of getting from the house to the spring without going anywhere near the spring path, even to the extent of paddling up the stream-bed for the final few feet if the paved area at the springhead were iced up.

So down went the paving stones again—this time in a smooth, nicely curved path from the back door to the spring. And I have swung along this path with my buckets ever since.

3. Weeds

What is a weed? I have read that the word 'weed' comes from the Anglo-Saxon word *weod*, which means 'herb', or 'small plant'. So a weed is a herb is a plant is a weed. However, some people do not find the subject at all confusing. A weed is any plant they don't like, or any plant which they suspect, however slightly, might be a wild plant, not a garden plant. We once knew someone who grew in her garden, and enjoyed, a whole bed of nettle-leaved bell-flower. Then one day we pointed out to her that it was, in fact, a wild flower. She was horrified, and the following day dug it all out and burnt it.

The term 'wild flower' is also open to argument. I suspect that a lot of people sort it out to themselves like this . . . Garden flowers are, well, garden flowers; everyone knows garden flowers. Wild flowers are primroses, violets, bluebells and dog-roses; weeds are buttercups, daisies, dandelions, docks, nettles and groundsel, plus all the other things they don't know the names of.

A few years ago I telephoned the local council to complain furiously about their policy of spraying the roadsides with poison. It had been an unusually mild and lush springtime and my cycle ride to Llanrwst in the month of May had been sheer delight. Spinning down through the woods, the scent of fresh-ness and sweet blossom was almost intoxicating. Coming home again—a long uphill climb—I was glad of the excuse to walk so that I could look, and linger, and touch and sniff the delicate blossoms, soft petals and smooth leaves. When I travelled that way a week later it was a different scene. A four-foot-wide band of brown, rank death lined the road. Nothing stood upright except the stiff, blackening stalks of nettle and dock. I couldn't wait to get to a telephone kiosk. 'Do you ever go and *look* at the results of your spraying?' I shouted at the official who was hold-

ing the telephone at the other end. 'You are in charge of some
of the most beautiful roads in the county—God help us—and
this is what you do to them! Do you realize what you have
destroyed?' I ranted on, 'I've never seen that road looking
lovelier; magnificent hedge-parsley, wood anemones, wild
strawberries and whinberries. What chance is there now for any
of these plants to bear fruit this autumn? What about the
cow-wheat? There were whole banks of bell-flowers, campions,
St. John's wort, Welsh poppies and yellow pimpernel; and
where are the ragged robins and mollyblobs now?' I paused
for breath and my listener hastily got a word in. 'I'm very
sorry, madam. Really that must have been accidental. They
were only supposed to spray the *weeds. . . .*'

I suppose the best definition of a weed is *any* wild plant that
is not wanted. By this definition we have very few weeds at
Hafod.

In the early days, when we were preparing ground for growing crops, I was so intent upon getting a piece of earth ready to
receive our seeds that I didn't take a lot of notice of the vegetation I was digging out. I worked methodically. Compostable
stuff went in one pile, stones in another and burnable rubbish
and roots in another. I worked until the particular patch I was
turning over was completely clear, then I carted away the dug-
out foliage, stones, rubbish and roots and dumped them in
appropriate places. Then I straightened my back and looked
proudly at my nice tidy patch of soil. One day I came across
Alan scraping off his spade, having apparently completed a
piece of ground clearance, yet a small cluster of straggling
greenery sat jauntily in the centre. 'What's that?' I said, pointing an accusing finger. 'I don't know,' he replied, 'which is why
I've left it.'

The making of a garden in a sensitive manner, having complete regard for everything that grows and lives there, is a
philosophy that is as natural as breathing to Alan. I have come
to learn it. It had never occurred to me before that a plant
should at least be identified before a decision as to its fate is
made. And as my knowledge of plants is much sketchier than

Alan's, I am continually asking him to come and look at something before I yank it out. Once I thought I had discovered something very rare. I had certainly never seen any seedling like it. I nurtured it in the beetroot bed, until Alan found out. 'That's shepherd's purse,' he said, pulling it out, 'We've loads of it all over the place, and the one patch of ground where we don't want it growing is in the vegetable garden.'

Alan makes decisions by instinct. He follows no set of rules that he could quote. The fate of each plant is decided individually. And if you think this must make him a very slow and laborious gardener, you would be wrong. Normally he either works fast and furiously, or not at all. Take, for example, clearing grass in the wych-elm plot. For most of the year we allow this patch to grow without interference; but my washing hangs in the wych-elm plot (on a line that runs from the wych-elm to the old privy) and occasionally the stage is reached where soaring bracken, dock and grass get in the way of the sheets and shirts. Then I protest, and Alan moves in with his sickle to clear a patch near the washing line. Bracken, dock, Yorkshire fog grass and nettles predominate, and Alan will wade in slashing—apparently indiscriminately. Suddenly he will stop. He will drop his sickle, kneel down, and pull at the grass with his hands. And there, sitting meekly in an area of hand-cleared ground will be An Interesting Plant. Amongst all those millions of grasses, stalks and fronds, Alan will have noticed two stems and half a dozen leaves that are different.

Usually he is ruthless with the weeds in the vegetable seed-bed. Nothing must be allowed to interfere with food production. But once our vegetables are growing strongly, and well able to look after themselves, then the weeds will be left alone, unless a particular one gets too aggressive and is likely to swamp a neighbouring vegetable. Not only does this practice allow us to enjoy observing the weeds in the vegetable garden, but we have also found it to be a good idea for several practical reasons. To begin with, a good cover of small weeds stops the ground from drying out so much during very hot weather, and also prevents soil being blown away during windy weather or washed away during flood-type wet weather. Moreover, under storm conditions, a stand of tall, strong weeds will protect small, weak vegetables. Certainly tall weeds will also keep the sun off small vegetables, but it is surprising just how tolerant most vegetables are of being nudged on all sides by sturdy weeds. As we often have to leave the cottage for several weeks at a time, our garden sometimes becomes too weedy even for us, yet we have only once lost a crop through the encroachment of a weed (namely chickweed, which smothered the peas). When we return to Hafod after a period away at work, one of our first actions is to inspect the vegetable garden—somewhat fearfully. But we are always relieved to find that very few vegetables have suffered. Once—because of a combination of circumstances involving working away from home followed by illness in the family—we were away from Hafod for three months during the summer. It had been a very dry three months, and we returned to find the vegetable garden waist high in weeds. We waded into it gloomily, wondering what, if anything, could be salvaged. Not a vegetable was to be seen . . . until we started investigating. First of all we found the kale, doing quite nicely, thank you. Then we found a row of beetroot, looking rather sickly and with many gaps, but still quite a few hopefully alive. Next the potatoes came into view. Admittedly all the haulms collapsed as we removed the weeds from around them, but they recovered and produced a fair crop of spuds later in the year. But the biggest surprise (as readers of *Hovel in the Hills* will remember) was the onion bed. The onions— lovers of sunshine and openness—were completely covered by the heftiest, toughest, and most spread-eagled of weeds. Yet we cleared back all this growth to find the biggest and best crop of onions we have ever lifted—before or since. The following few weeks were dry and sunny, and the onions ripened beautifully and stored perfectly that winter.

Now, here are a few more reasons to justify the weeds. Pest food, for example. If you think that feeding pests is a crazy notion, then let me explain. Leaving aside for the moment the argument that, as a weed is but a plant in the wrong place, so a pest is but an animal in the wrong place, just think for a moment about those pests that you are so desperately trying to get rid of. You presumably hate them because they eat your crops; if they didn't eat your crops you wouldn't bother about them. So the obvious answer is to ensure that your pests have something to eat other than your vegetables.

Take wireworms, for instance. Wireworms live mostly under grass turf. Any gardening book will tell you that if you are making a vegetable garden out of a previously grassed area then you are likely to have trouble with wireworms. Presumably wireworms live under grass turf because they like to eat grass roots. If you come along and remove all the grass, then plant potatoes, the wireworm, deprived of his normal food, has no alternative but to eat your potatoes. (All right; so it's better to remove the wireworms as well as the grass. But you know perfectly well that you'll never manage it. Try as hard as you like, there will be wireworms there for a long time.) Now, if you leave plenty of grass in and around your potato patch, no wireworm is going to change his diet to eat your potatoes when he can have his ideal meal of grass roots. (I am speaking from practical experience. We have never had trouble with wireworms when growing potatoes in our field.)

Do you have trouble with bullfinches? We never do, and yet small parties of these delightful pests pass through our garden during the late winter days, just as the fruit buds are forming on the gooseberry and blackcurrant bushes. We once spent several hours during a sunny February afternoon watching a pair of hungry bullfinches feeding amongst the budding gooseberry bushes. They weren't the slightest bit interested in the fruit buds, they were gorging themselves upon the massive seed heads of a mixed stand of docks and sorrel, still heavy with seed after an exceptionally mild winter.

We have found no one else who shares our views on weeds, and if we get any visitors when the garden is supporting a particularly prolific crop of them, our visitors don't know whether to sympathize or criticize. Together we all stare at the garden in embarrassed silence. Unless the visitor happens to be Muriel, that is. Muriel, a single, retired lady who came to live in the area a few years ago, is never embarrassed or silent.

When Muriel first moved into Bryn Certan (a cottage similar to Hafod, but near Llanrwst) we went down to introduce ourselves as we thought that, being English and living alone, she might like some help and reassurance about life in a cottage on the moors. We thought she might like to be told about local conditions and people. We were wrong. Muriel didn't *receive* information from anyone; she *gave* it. Mind you, she also gave her services to the local meals-on-wheels brigade, her home-made jam to the chapel bazaar, her extremely high-quality cast-off walking jackets to me, and cups of tea to any passing hiker. But Muriel was a retired schoolteacher, and forty years in front of the blackboard had made their mark. She astounded us first of all by telling us who we were before we had a chance to introduce ourselves. 'Oh, I've gone into it all,' she explained, 'I have looked up everybody locally in the Register of Electors, and made a note of the names and addresses of all my neighbours.'

Botany was Muriel's subject and she is very knowledgeable on all forms of plant life. She is always curious to see what we are growing at Hafod, but she has an infuriating habit of never listening to a thing we say. A conversation with Muriel in the garden will go something like this:

Muriel: (nudging with her toe a clump of wood-sorrel) 'Ah, I see you have some *Oxalis acetosella.*'

Me: 'Yes, it's pretty, isn't it. We eat quite a bit of it.'

Muriel: 'Notice that the leaves are radical and the scapes single-flowered. They rise from a creeping rhizome and you will find that the capsules are five-angled ovoids.'

Me: 'Is that so? I didn't know that. But it's jolly good to garnish a sandwich.'

Muriel: 'The American Indians used to feed their horses with the crushed roots. It grows in woods and other shady situations.'

Me: 'Well, it certainly grows well in this situation, and *we* like it in salads.'

Muriel: (bending down, yanking it out and throwing it into the
    hedge) 'It is, of course, a common weed, but you can in
    fact eat it.'

Needless to say, Muriel doesn't grow weeds in *her* garden.
They are of academic interest only and are despatched quite
ruthlessly. She once tackled a large stand of nettles between her
garden wall and the road with a poison spray. The nettles,
previously large, untidy and dark green, were now large, untidy
and dark brown. They stayed that way for about a fortnight
before Muriel, seemingly fed up with the sight of them, set to
with garden shears and chopped them all down—which she
could have done in the first place, thus saving herself money,
energy and frustration. But Muriel was not convinced. 'They
were *supposed* to die back,' she said, frowning over the label on
the bottle of poison. (This complete and utter belief in the
written word is another of Muriel's inflexibilities, and her
botanical reference books would, of course, never be doubted.
'Wych-elms don't have suckers,' she once declared, whilst
staring at the bunch of wych-elm suckers sprouting from the
bank beneath the Hafod wych-elm.) Even Muriel's 'Wonder
Weeder Bar' didn't make her have second thoughts about the
wisdom of introducing poison to the garden. This particular
gimmick was a selective herbicide in the form of a waxy bar
which one dragged across a lawn in order to kill the weeds.
Muriel had two very large lawns which she was determined to
keep weed free. The Wonder Weeder bar was guaranteed to
remove all forms of plant life except the particular grasses
wanted in a lawn, and I must admit that it worked. Muriel's
lawns had nothing growing in them except grass. True, there
were many little brown patches where previously there had
been daisies, clovers, plantains and other noxious weeds, but
Muriel was quite happy. 'It will soon all grass over,' she declared. Two years later Muriel's vegetable garden was a
disaster. There was only sporadic and sickly germination of
many of her seeds, and there was no sign of any life whatsoever
in her potato patch, her broad bean bed or her line of peas.
Nothing. Absolutely nothing. It was some time before the an-

swer occurred to her. Compost. All her lawn cuttings had been put on to her compost heaps, and the compost had been distributed lavishly around her vegetable garden in the spring. But did this episode put Muriel off poisons? No. It simply put her off compost. She now buys chemical fertilizers.

Returning to Hafod, where the native plants grow saucily, and largely unhindered, I now come to another good reason for allowing weeds to thrive in the garden. They feed us.

To cultivate vegetables on an exposed moorland, with thin, poor, acid soil at an elevation of 1,000 feet above sea-level is almost a gesture of hope, rather than an action of positive intention. The fact that, to a large extent, we have succeeded is due mainly to our non-stop efforts to improve the soil and to provide shelter by planting trees. But our crops are always in danger. At any time of the year they could be destroyed by extreme weather conditions. The plants that have been growing here for centuries know all about storm, flood, frost, snow and drought and have built-in survival capabilities, whereas our vegetables—many of which are grown from seed that probably last saw the light of day in some lush, warm, sunny clime—are liable to curl up and die if prolonged nasty weather hits them.* It was obvious, therefore, if only for reasons of pure common sense, to find out which of the native plants were edible and palatable.

We have some reference books on the subject which I consult every time we are about to try something new, but Alan just chews anything that takes his fancy. As a child he wandered freely in the open countryside and woodland that bordered the new housing estate where he was brought up, and he claims to have been nibbling at wild greenery and fruit ever since the age of four. Consequently, he seems to have developed a sort of instinct which tells him what is liable to taste good, and what isn't. I don't recommend this behaviour to anyone else, and I really wish Alan would be a bit more cautious. What usually

* Over the years, several varieties of kale, parsley, thyme and marjoram—also the land-cress and lambs' lettuce—have got used to the weather and have naturalized themselves here. They are now part of the Hafod natural growth.

happens is this: Alan will identify a plant in the garden, and claim that it's good to eat. I will rush off into the house to check up in one of our books—and in the meantime he's eaten it. So far he has survived.

Normally we eat weeds uncooked, in salads or in sandwiches. We eat them all year round, but we are particularly grateful for them in the winter and early spring when there is very little to eat in the way of salad greenery in the vegetable garden. (There is always kale, but I can't really contemplate eating platefuls of it raw, day after day.) Some weeds are not very tasty, but nice and soft and juicy; others are tougher and with strong flavours. So we find the best way of eating them is to take a selection, cut into small pieces and mix in a bowl with a spoonful of salad cream. This is our basic green salad. Served with tomatoes, beetroot, hard-boiled eggs, cheese, or anything else suitable that we might have, it is now a regular part of our diet. Friends who have come to stay have tried it, first of all cautiously, and then enthusiastically. They have nicknamed the dish 'Wild West Salad' and now thoroughly recommend it.

We have investigated the eating possibilities of most of the Hafod weeds and feel we are in a position to give advice to others. In the following paragraphs are some brief details of a few of the commonest edible weeds. I have given description of plants only when they may be confused with others. If you are not already familiar with them I suggest you consult an appropriate reference book. Where I have information on the alleged medicinal and/or nutrient content of the plant, I have quoted it, but I can make no personal claim to knowledge of the subject; I only know that these plants are good to eat—and we eat them.

Chickweed *(Stellaria media)*

Light-green, delicate, creeping plant with long, soft, almost translucent stems and small, white, starry flowers. The leaves are small and lilac-leaf shaped. Appears readily on bare earth. Do not confuse with other chickweeds and stitchworts.

I start with chickweed because it is our favourite wild plant food. Its seeds germinate all the year round and we have even found it flourishing under snow. It has a mild flavour and we now prefer it to watercress. (It used to be grown commercially and sold as a salad cress. It grows so well and so easily that I cannot think why this trade has died out.)

It is rich in copper and iron, and claims have been made that a brew of boiled chickweed will help relieve constipation and any form of stomach upset and also makes an excellent eye lotion.

We think that chickweed should be encouraged in all gardens, but kept under control because it can kill other plants by smothering them—as we learned to our cost. Having become enthusiastic chickweed eaters (and liking to see its pretty, trailing growth around the garden) we weren't at all concerned when we noticed it climbing up the pea sticks along with the peas. Peas and chickweed growing together—how nice! Then we went away and left it for a few weeks. When we came back there was a gigantic crop of chickweed all over a row of dead pea plants.

Red Clover *(Trifolium pratense)*   **White Clover** *(T. repens)*

Plants contain nitrogen and sodium. Clover tea was an old remedy for all coughs and catarrh. We eat the flowers, which are very slightly sweet.

Dandelion *(Taraxacum officinale)*

Contains copper, iron and potassium and also large quantities of vitamins C and A. A decoction of the leaves and roots is supposed to help relieve eczema and other skin disorders. We eat only the leaves. They have a slightly bitter taste so we do not have more than three or four leaves, well chopped, in a salad mixture.

Groundsel *(Senicio vulgaris)*

Small, yellow flowers like tiny, worn-out shaving brushes. Leaves grey-green and notched. Grows all year round. Contains iron. Was once used as a remedy for scurvy. We find it has no particular taste, but as it is one of those plants that always seem to be around we usually take a few leaves for the salad.

Sow, or milk, thistle *(Sonchus oleraceus)*

Yellow, thistle-like flowers, 'polished' leaves with roughly serrated edges. This plant can grow to four feet or so, but we only take young leaves from small plants. The leaves and stem exude milky juice when broken. Rich in minerals and vitamin C. (A favourite salad vegetable of the Romans.) Some claim is made that the milk juice is good for the complexion. Mild but pleasant taste.

Sorrel *(Rumex acetosa)*

Flowers are reddish and grow in tall spikes. (Do not confuse with sheep's sorrel or common dock.) Leaves are spear-shaped. Has a slightly acid flavour, and adds a vinegary 'bite' to the salad mixture.

The above weeds are very common and some of them probably appear from time to time in *your* garden. Why not try eating them, instead of destroying them? And whilst wandering around your garden gathering weeds, pick some mint leaves, thyme, sage and parsley to add to your salad; if you have some primroses, borage or lady's smock growing nearby, then add a few of their flowers. What about the raspberries, blackcurrants, blackberries and strawberries? Early in the spring the new, young leaves are pleasant to eat. All these plants, and others, find their way, in season, into the 'Wild West' salad bowl.

There are three well-known weeds, renowned for their nutritional qualities, that we have never got on with: goosefoot,
couch-grass and stinging nettle.

The goosefoot family (Chenopodiaceae) are supposed to
contain more vitamin B, iron and protein than cabbage or
spinach. But as we find the leaves fiddly to gather, and tasteless
to eat, we don't bother with them.

Couch-grass (*Agropyron repens*) is that persistent, tough grass
that spreads rapidly by means of long, ivory-coloured roots. It
is a great nuisance in any garden, and I wish we could eat our
way through it, but we find the roots tough and tasteless. They
are said to be a rich source of potassium and many other de-
sirable nutrients. This is the grass that dogs sometimes eat
when they are feeling unwell, and I have read that an infusion
of the roots produces a tea that will relieve rheumatism, gout
and cystitis. This may be true (and if we suffered from rheumatism, gout or cystitis perhaps we would be persuaded to try
some) but for us couch-grass has no use. We daren't compost the
roots (they would just go on growing) so we burn them.

Stinging nettles are another failure so far as we are concerned. They are of no trouble to us (roots can be removed
easily enough) and we leave plenty of them around for the
benefit of butterflies, but we have never enjoyed eating them.
The usually recommended way of eating stinging nettles is to
boil them briefly (like spinach) and serve with butter. I found
that a large saucepan squashed full of nettles (that took a long
time to pick) boiled down to a couple of tablespoonfuls of
greenery that had no particular taste and didn't feel very
pleasant in my mouth. We have never tried nettle soup, and
I should think that it tastes rather insipid, but I sometimes add
a handful of young nettle tops to a mixed vegetable soup.

We once read that a stand of nettles growing around the
blackcurrant bushes would encourage them to grow lustily and
fruit prolifically. As there was a large patch of nettles near the
stable and we happened to have several blackcurrant cuttings
that needed encouragement, we decided to experiment. Certainly the soil just outside the stable looked very nourishing (no

doubt thanks to generations of horse-droppings, which probably accounted for the very healthy nettles) so Alan waded in amongst them and planted sixteen rooted cuttings. For about two years these cuttings just survived, producing a few berries only. Now (about eight years later) they are healthy but small-sized bushes, producing a fair crop of blackcurrants. But, supposing we had removed all the nettles and planted these bushes in that same rich soil; would they have grown much bigger and produced much more fruit? Whether or not this is the case, we can say quite definitely that there is at least one benefit to be gained by planting blackcurrant bushes in a stand of nettles: the fruit is given almost complete protection from the birds. As the nettles grow as high as the bushes, most of the fruit is concealed, and the few berries on the top of the bushes are practically unobtainable—if you happen to be a bird and want somewhere firm to put your feet. I have watched a black bird flapping frustratedly around the tops of the nettles, trying, but failing, to find a foothold.

Admittedly, the stinging nettles make the gathering of the crop an awkward job for us, but on the whole we consider it was a worthwhile experiment and we have no intention of moving the bushes now. They are obviously quite happy there.

Protecting a fruit crop may be *our* only use for stinging nettles; other people do other things with them—like making beer.

I have a friend who makes very good nettle beer. (*She* says it is good. . . . There has never been any left for us to try when we have called!) It is apparently very lively, has to be kept well screwed down, and is recommended for cheering up melancholy moments.

Here is her recipe:

BRENDA'S NETTLE BEER
    2 lb young nettles
        (set aside a couple of hours for
        gathering this lot—you'll need it!)
    2 lemons

1 lb brown sugar
1 gallon water
1 oz cream of tartar
1 oz yeast

Put nettles and water into large pan and boil for about 15 minutes. Strain off into a bowl into which you have already put the grated lemon peel and juice, sugar and cream of tartar.

Give a good stir and when it is cool add the yeast and give it another good stir. Keep it covered with a cloth and leave standing in a warm room for 3 days. Strain, bottle and cork down and leave it for at least a week before drinking.

Cheers!

4. Food from the wilderness

We wanted to grow fruit and vegetables. We also wanted to introduce more trees, shrubs and flowers; and we wanted to play around with rocks and pathways. This would mean destroying some plants and interfering with the lives of some animals, so we had to do it thoughtfully. We started by looking around to see what was growing here already.

We have never identified all the grasses. There is a large variety of them—some coarse and tufty, and some smooth, soft and smothery but (apart from cock's-foot) we have none of the lush, nourishing grasses found in the lowlands. We have most of the wild flowers you would expect to find in this sort of situation and, when we fenced off a corner of the field in order to make it part of the garden, we discovered that even such a harmless interference as the putting up of a fence will change a community of plants. The field (which is grazed by a neighbour's sheep) has probably been a close-nibbled turf for centuries, and tiny tormentil, tom thumbs, milkwort and heartsease smile up at us from the very short grass, together with yarrow and harebells. The piece of former field—now enclosed by the garden fence—grows grass which is sometimes shoulder high. The heartsease, yarrow and harebells are still there but, within this fenced-off area, we have lost the tormentil, tom thumbs and milkwort.

We were glad that we had some trees, and were surprised at the height of the two mature ash trees and the wych-elm. We are just about on the tree-line here and there are no other trees of such size anywhere near us.

I love all trees, but if I had to choose a favourite I think it would be the impudent elder—and I was delighted to find two growing at Hafod. The elder grows anywhere and everywhere. You can't keep it down; it absolutely insists upon growing in field, forest, wasteland, garden and factory yard and on walls and mountain sides. With its fragrant, dancing blossoms in summer and its succulent berries in autumn, its very persistence seems to represent hope for the future. When the Last Trumpet sounds (or when that Last Button is pushed), I somehow feel that, out of the ashes, will sprout an elder tree.

We love the elder but are well aware that not many other people do. It is noticeable that when woodland is being cleared for housing sites it sometimes happens that a builder with imagination will preserve certain trees to add a touch of interest and natural beauty to his finished estate. In this way some fine specimens of birch, chestnut and sycamore have been saved— but no such reprieve is ever granted to the common elder (*Sambucus nigra*), a tree inevitably destined for the first shove of the bulldozer. Moreover, if by some accident an elder is left to flourish in someone's brand-new plot, the new houseowner will more than likely have it rooted out before the men have finished moving in the furniture.

Why this attractive and useful little tree should have acquired such widespread dislike is puzzling, especially as there are so many excellent reasons for having one. To begin with, it is our most rapidly growing tree in its early years, and any bit of living wood will readily take root. For an almost-instant live screen between you and your neighbour a hedge of elder cuttings takes a lot of beating. Not only does it grow fast, it also grows anywhere, never grows very tall and will withstand the severest weather, including salt-laden gales. It is happiest in full light and really thrives on soils rich in nitrogen, which is why it is often found rampaging away upon rubbish heaps and rabbit warrens. It is said that the elder is the only tree that rabbits won't eat, so here is another reason for recommending it to the would-be hedge grower.

Perhaps the most significant quality of the elder today is its absolute resistance to the worst possible sorts of pollution. There are sturdy elders to be seen flourishing on a railway embankment adjoining a chemical works in Manchester . . . and atmospheres don't come much thicker than that!

The elder has other uses which were certainly valued by our forefathers, even if they remain unappreciated ·today. The clusters of white flowers can be used for flavouring milk or stewed fruit, adding to fritters, making still and sparkling wines and soothing ointment (a fact that was recognized by at least one manufacturer of ointments who made free with the tree's Latin generic title *Sambucus* when fixing on a trade name). The juicy, purple berries make chutneys, syrups and wines, whilst an infusion of the leaves makes a lotion to protect the skin against attack by mosquitoes and midges. If you are in need of fire bellows, flute, whistle, blow-gun or pop-gun, you'll find the young wood of the elder just right for the job as the central core of pith can be easily removed; and sufferers from rheumatics, nerves, dropsy, gout or epilepsy might try a brew of elder roots and bark.

Anyone still unconvinced of the elder's value will surely relent upon learning that an elder in your garden will frustrate witches, protect your cattle from the evil eye, guard the dead in the churchyard (and keep them there) and is an infallible protection against all curses, maledictions, lightning and thunderbolt. Show me the insurance policy that equals that!

On a cautionary note, you are warned never to use an elder switch to beat your child, as his growth may be stunted; and to burn elder is to invite extreme bad luck. Gypsies apparently consider elder to be sacred, and for this reason will never burn it on their fires. The fact that it makes rotten kindling and provides little heat is another good reason.

After reading this, perhaps anyone lucky enough to have an elder tree growing at hand will lay down his axe and give the tree a chance to prove its worth. A trial of the following recipes could be a start:

ELDERFLOWER CHAMPAGNE
5 or 6 heads elderflowers
white wine vinegar, 2 tablespoonfuls
white sugar, 2 lb
cold water, 8 pints

hot water, 4 pints
lemons, 2

Pick the heads when in full bloom and put into a bowl with the vinegar, cut-up lemon rind and juice, and sugar dissolved in the hot water. Add the cold water and leave for 3 days, occasionally giving a good stir. Strain into strong bottles, cork firmly and lay them on their sides. After about 2 weeks it should be sparkling and ready to drink.

I think I should add that there is something mysterious about this recipe. (Indeed, isn't there something mysterious about all home-brew recipes?) When I made this champagne in Bristol with normal city tap-water and Bristol elderflowers the drink was a complete success. But made with Hafod elderflowers and Hafod spring water all I get is a completely flat, albeit sweet and fragrant, drink. Absolutely no fizz whatsoever. Something to do with the acid water perhaps? I can offer no explanation.

ELDERBERRY WINE

There is an old lady, living a few miles away from us, whom we consider to be a champion wine maker. She knows nothing about pectin-destroying enzymes, lactic acid bacteria, or Camden tablets, and she wouldn't know what to do with an inverted U-tube air lock if you gave her one. Neither is she too fussy about sterilization. She makes wine in old beer bottles, vinegar bottles and lemonade bottles. And she stacks them on her kitchen window-sill along with the washing-up liquid, dish mop and packets of soap powder. These bottles pop and gurgle alongside dingy net curtains hanging with dead flies, and in front of panes of glass thick with cobwebs. Her wine is superb. It is smooth and glowing; it is mild to the tongue, but with a suggestion of hidden power in its fruity depths. After a glass of old Amy's wine you come away thinking the world is a very nice place. Her favourite drink is pea-pod wine, and she has countless bottles of this stacked away in various cupboards around the house. But she also makes elderberry wine—and this is the one that I like best. When I was last there I asked her to let me have her recipe. Here it is, exactly as she wrote it down:

> '4 lbs of berries
> 1 gallon of water

Strip berries from stalks. Pour on one gallon of boiling water to each four pounds of berries. Let this stand for twenty four hours. Then bruises them well an strain. Measure up liquid an to each gallon allow three pounds of sugar. Take a little of this an boil up with

> 1 lb raisins,
> $\frac{1}{2}$ oz cloves
> 1 oz root ginger well brused
> an 2 sliced lemon

Pour back on to the other, an strain again. Set with one oz. yeast. Allow this to stand for a few days then take off cap an strain again. Put in casks or bottles keeping fulled up until fermentation finishes. After bung down tightly.'

ELDERBERRY SAUCE

I once followed a recipe for elderberry pickle. It smelt delicious when I was making it, and it looked good in the jars, but it was a great disappointment when we came to eat it. The taste was fine, but the tiny elderberry seeds were an infuriating nuisance. It was like eating a good, fruity pickle into which someone had put two handfuls of sand. I decided to sieve it. I spooned it all out of the jars again and pressed it through a strainer. A long, messy job, but well worth while. The resulting sauce was delicious, and we like it with bacon and egg, cheese dishes and in cold meat sandwiches. I decided to make another batch of elderberry 'sauce', this time doing the straining at a more convenient time. It was a complete success; so here is my recipe:

> 2 medium-sized onions
> 1 lb elderberries
> 2 level tablespoonfuls Barbados sugar
> $\frac{1}{2}$ level teaspoonful ground ginger

> 1 level teaspoonful ground mixed spice
> $\frac{1}{2}$ pint vinegar
> pinch of salt

Place washed and rinsed jars in slow oven to heat. Skin the onions and chop finely. Wash the elderberries, remove the stalks. Put berries in a basin and mash them well. Put in an enamel or aluminium pan. (Do not use a copper pan.) Add the onion, sugar, ginger, mixed spice, vinegar and salt. Bring to the boil. Cook *very slowly* for 40–50 minutes, stirring frequently to prevent the sauce burning. Pour through strainer into jug. (My strainer is like a very large tea strainer, and I find that this mixture can be helped through the strainer by pressing it with the back of a wooden spoon.) By the time you have finished doing this the sauce mixture will have cooled, so put it back into the pan, bring it to the boil again. Then put hot sauce into the hot jars and put on tops immediately.

GRANNY'S ELDERFLOWER OINTMENT
Refined petroleum jelly (such as Vaseline)
Elderflowers

Put the jelly into a saucepan with as many elderflowers (minus stems) as can be pressed into it. Simmer gently for about 1 hour. Whilst very hot, strain into small pots. This ointment is ready for use as soon as cold and is excellent for chapped or rough hands. (Please don't write and tell me that refined petroleum jelly will soothe chapped or rough hands without the bother of including the elderflowers. I know; but, if nothing else, the elderflowers make it smell a bit nicer!)

Finally, no one stewing gooseberries with an elder tree nearby should fail to drop a few heads of flowers into the fruit. The flowerheads (remove before serving) give the fruit an exquisite vanilla-like flavour. Elder blossoms can be added to gooseberries when bottling, prettily decorating the fruit in the jar as well as flavouring it.

Those who still consider the common elder to be not only

common, but also vulgar, may be interested to know that the tree has some respectable cousins which should be acceptable even to gardening purists. Some of these cultivated members of the *Sambucus* genus are:

S. canadensis 'Maxima'—one of the American elderberries, with large leaves and very large clusters of flowers

S. nigra 'Aurea'   —the golden-leaved elder

S. nigra 'Lacineata'   —a cut-leaved form of the golden-leaved elder

S. racemosa   —the red-berried elder

Their flowers may be suitable for Granny's ointment, but it should be noted that these trees carry no guarantee whatsoever of mystical protection. Plant any of them in your garden and you must make alternative arrangements to ward off any passing coven.

We, needless to say, are perfectly happy with *Sambucus nigra*, and we have planted cuttings from our two trees all around Hafod. Nearly every cutting has taken and is flourishing happily . . . and we haven't seen a witch in years!

Another tree that tolerates a smoky atmosphere and poor soil is the rowan, which is why it is seen in suburbia as well as upon mountain sides. In the lowlands it grows into a well-shaped tree, nicely proportioned and with a straight trunk but, to me, the rowan seems more at home in the wilderness, defying storms and blizzards, even though it sometimes bends through 90 degrees in the attempt. There were two rowans here when we came to Hafod. There are now so many that we have lost count of them. They are sprouting up all over the place. A rowan seed even germinated in a fork of our biggest elder tree. We watched, curiously, over a couple of years as it grew into a sturdy little sapling, but it died during the drought. (Incidentally, a large fern and a herb robert are also growing in forks of the elder. Both the elder and its lodgers seem to be quite happy with this arrangement.)

We notice that a rowan sapling will produce flowers and berries even when it is very young and small. We are very glad of this abundance of berries around the place because I like to gather some each year to make rowanberry jelly, and it is always a race to get some from the tree before the mistle thrushes and starlings take them all. We don't often have resident starlings, but flocks of them swoop over each evening on their way from somewhere to somewhere else in that dramatic, orderly way in which starlings go about. When they are passing this way at rowanberry time a certain disorder can be seen amongst their ranks. One of the flock spots the rowanberries gleaming like tiny, red jewels all over the tree. The brakes are applied; there is confusion; an exchange of a few, squawked swear-words; a sudden change of command; then the whole flock wheels around and alights with greedy delight upon the tree. There is much squabbling, chattering and gobbling down of berries. Before dusk falls they take off again. One of them has made the decision; the word is given; the last berries are choked down, and then swoosh! They are off, swarming across the sky into the sunset. And I make up my mind that the very next day—before the next starling contingent passes over—I must go out to gather my rowanberries for this year's jelly.

ROWANBERRY JELLY

You will need 1 pint of water for every 4 lb of rowanberries. Simmer berries with the water. When soft, strain through a jelly-bag, and leave to drip overnight. To each pint of juice add 12 oz of sugar (for a sharp jelly) or 1 lb of sugar (for a sweeter jelly) and the juice of 1 large or 2 small lemons. Stir well until the sugar has dissolved, then boil rapidly until setting point is reached. (I find that it takes 20–30 minutes to set, and that 4 lb of rowanberries will yield about $2\frac{3}{4}$ lb of jelly.)

I discovered rowanberry jelly whilst we were living in the city. The road outside our flat was lined with graceful rowan trees and when, in the late summer, they produced an abundance of red berries I searched through my cookery books to find out what, if anything, could be done with them. Having found the recipe for rowanberry jelly, I wanted to try it. But how was I to get the berries? Take out the step-ladder and just pick what I wanted? I felt sure that someone would telephone the police and complain that a vandal was at work. I decided to ring the local council and ask for permission. The town hall official to whom I spoke was perplexed. My request was quite polite and straightforward. Could I please pick some berries from the rowan tree growing in the road outside the house. 'What do you want them for?' he asked suspiciously. He seemed unconvinced by my answer, but eventually gave his permission. (He wasn't very happy about it. I could almost hear his doubtful thoughts. . . . 'What if *everybody* wants to have some?')

We were so pleased with the jelly that we now make some every year. We use it with lamb, pork or chicken, and Alan likes great dollops of it on a hunk of bread and cheese. One year he made some spiced rowanberry jelly, simply by pouring off some of the jelly before it had reached setting point and adding a spoonful of ground ginger and a spoonful of mixed spice. He claims that it made a more interesting jelly, but I prefer it plain.

The Hafod wilderness—becoming more and more fruitful with the increase of rowan and elder trees—also includes 280 yards or so of mixed hawthorn and blackberry hedge. The haws I leave to the birds, who eat them half-heartedly but spread the seed around liberally. Consequently we now have a few little hawthorn trees sprouting up around the place.

Caring for a long length of hawthorn hedge is quite a laborious job. We are not concerned about the raggle-taggle appearance of it, but when long, barbed branches stick out across the road we feel we have to do something about it. Moreover, we know that the density of the hedge is likely to be improved by frequent and careful cutting. Originally these ancient hawthorns were cut and laid in traditional hedge fashion, but they have been neglected for the past fifty years or so and some of them have become quite substantial trees. The best we can do is to keep them trimmed and put other hedging plants in the gaps. Some of the acorns we sowed a few years ago are now 3-foot-high oak trees, and, of course, our elder cuttings are also filling quite a few hedge spaces. (Incidentally, hedge cutting is another one of those his/hers occupations. His job is wielding the long-handled pruners, saw and billhook, then dropping the brushwood upon the ground. Her job is trailing on behind, picking it all up, carting it into the field, and setting fire to it. Both of us get very scratched in the process.)

We are happy to leave the haws to the birds, but we certainly try to pick the blackberries before they do. When the blackberries start ripening (usually at the end of August) I am out most days with my bowl to make sure of them. We eat them raw, or simmered gently with a small amount of sugar (quite often dished up with rice pudding—delicious!). I make tarts, pies and puddings from blackberries; I bottle them, and I make jam. The blackberry harvest is an important one to us, and I gather as many as I can. I am very mean, possessive and self-righteous about the blackberries in our hedge. But I am very light-hearted when it comes to pinching them from other people's hedges. At blackberry time I always have a bag attached to my cycle handlebars, and when trudging up the hill from Llanrwst I can usually manage to fill it with blackberries from the hedges I pass on the way. I once arrived home with my handlebar bag full of blackberries, only to be astounded and furious to find a party of people who had stopped their car in the road and were *actually picking our blackberries*. The cheek of it! I refrained from comment as I cycled past, but went into the house thinking dark, glowering thoughts about people who steal other people's blackberries. I suppose my fury was understandable because, after all, those particular pickers were not observing the rules of the blackberry game. One should never be *caught* picking blackberries from a hedge that is within sight of the owner's house.

Picking whinberries* on the common is another matter. We have rights of turbary upon the common, but this doesn't give us entitlement to the whinberries that grow there. We pick them nevertheless, and we don't get upset if we see other people at it as well. Picking whinberries is such a long and tedious job that anyone who takes the trouble to pick them really earns the

* Bilberry or whortleberry (*Vaccinium myrtillus*).

fruit. The berries are tiny and so fiddly that it is only the knowledge of the exquisite flavour of whinberry pie that spurs us on.
I have not made jam with them. We have never been able to
pick enough. But one or two whinberry pies each year is enough
reward for several hours of hot and scratchy work grovelling
about on the common.

Another wild food we gather locally is fungi. In fact *I* do all
the gathering. Alan has no instincts when it comes to fungi—
only the instinct to leave well alone. He stands by, looking
doubtful but resigned, as I enthusiastically swoop on some
chanterelle in the woods, or a massive horse-mushroom or two
at the roadside.

We once found some fungi that looked very much like St.
George's mushrooms growing in a wood near Llanrwst. But as
(according to our book on the subject) the St. George's mushroom can be confused with the dangerously poisonous, red-
staining inocybe, we decided that we had better get some expert
advice before eating any. We took along a few samples to
Muriel. 'It certainly looks like the St. George's mushroom,' she
said, peering closely at one of the samples we had brought, 'See
how the gills are very crowded and attached to the stem with a
slight arch. But I think you had better leave these specimens
with me. I will do a spore test on them.' Encouraged by
Muriel's comments we went next day and filled a large bag
with these mushrooms, and called in to see Muriel on the way
home, to check her findings. 'Oh yes,' she said brightly, 'quite
definitely the St. George's mushroom. It is one of the genus
Tricholoma, and is edible and very good.' She handed us her
identification book, and pointed to the illustration and relevant
paragraph. 'They are excellent when fried or grilled,' she said,
quoting from the book. 'That's good,' I said, 'because we've
picked enough for all of us.' I opened my rucksack and started
to pull out a few choice specimens of the mushrooms and put
them on Muriel's kitchen table. 'Ah—well—I haven't actually
eaten any myself,' Muriel said hastily. 'Well, your book says
they are edible and good,' I argued, making quite a heap of
fungi upon her table, 'Excellent when fried or grilled,' I em-

phasized. 'Well, I'm not really very fond of fungi,' Muriel protested faintly, 'and anyway, I've already decided what I am having for my tea today.' 'They'll keep until tomorrow,' I said cheerfully, adding a few more to the pile.

We left Muriel standing unhappily beside her mushrooms. We went home and enjoyed an excellent meal of ours, but I have a faint suspicion that Muriel's might have been tipped into the rubbish bin.

One year (and one year only in the thirteen years we have been here) a large crop of horse-mushrooms appeared in our field. Although this particular fungus grows happily in the grass verges alongside the road, it had never before appeared on our ground and all through July and August we were picking masses of them. For some reason (known only to the mushrooms) this performance has never been repeated. But we always have plenty of puff-balls and are picking them throughout the summer. A lot of people are suspicious of puff-balls, and wouldn't dream of eating them. Yet, so far as I know, this particular fungus could not be confused with any poisonous one.* They are so plentiful about the countryside that it seems a shame so many of them are wasted. If picked young they are quite delicious when fried. A few years ago a giant puff-ball (weighing $6\frac{1}{4}$ lb and with a circumference of 42 inches) was found in a field at Chipping Sodbury. Fortunately its culinary value was appreciated locally. It was cut into $\frac{1}{2}$-inch slices, fried in oil and served as a meal to thirty-one people. No giant puff-balls have ever appeared in our field; we have only the common puff-ball, and find them no bigger than hen's eggs, but they are a welcome addition to the Hafod diet.

Another edible oddity we have found here is the pignut (*Conopodium majus*). It is a plant with frail, carrot-like leaves, and has tubers which lie two or three inches below the ground. These tubers are of the size and shape of hazel-nuts and taste a bit like raw chestnuts. Any we find we chop up and mix with our salad, or add to the mixture when making biscuits.

* Claire Lowenfeld in *Britain's Wild Larder* (Faber) describes and gives culinary uses of puff-balls.

It seems incredible to us that although wild foods are still obtainable from patches of wilderness up and down the country, most people choose to ignore them—apart from a blackberry expedition occasionally. I know a woman who lives in the middle of a wood. The trees nudge her garden fence, the thickets tangle over her chicken house and she has a half-mile walk to the main road. She is not happy in her wood. She hates the solitude and she hates the constant movement and rustling, but most of all she hates the expense of living in the country. 'They say it's cheap to live in the country, but I can't see it,' she grumbled to me the last time we met. It was an August morning, warm and gentle. We crunched our way through the twigs along her path, and paused by the wild raspberries and blackberries hanging at her gate. 'Every time I want a tin of fruit or a packet of firelighters,' she continued, 'it means a half-hour bus trip to town.'

Jams, jellies, wines, salads, sauces and mushrooms—all these foods were obtainable from the wilderness at Hafod *before we started planting anything.*

Not everyone locally was happy with our wilderness though. Dic's brother Dilwen (he organizes the financial side of their affairs) has a personality somewhat gloomier than Dic's, and when he saw the grasses growing long and lush inside our extended garden area he stared at it with a sort of grim disbelief. 'What are you going to do with it?' he asked. 'We shall plant some more trees,' we replied. 'What for?' he persisted in astonishment. 'We like trees,' we said. He shook his head slowly and grimly. 'Wicked,' he said quietly, 'Wicked'. 'What's wicked?' Alan asked. Dilwen shrugged his shoulders and turned away down the road. 'It's a wicked waste of grazing,' he called back over his shoulder.

5. The vegetable garden

Our main vegetable garden is an area roughly forty feet square lying behind the cottage on a south-west-facing slope. In the beginning we grew vegetables in small plots all around the place, most of them lurking behind the hawthorn hedges, but it was obviously sensible to set aside an area in which to concentrate upon vegetable growing. We gradually extended a plot behind the house, nibbling further and further up the hillside. Alan skimmed off the turf with a mattock. (These turves were put into piles and formed the basis of our original compost heaps.) The soil was obviously poor, and it became thinner and stonier the higher up the slope we cleared. We came to a point where we decided that we had reached the limit of a useful area for cultivation so we stopped. We have been improving the quality of this forty-foot-square plot ever since.

We knew that we would need shelter. We had planted Sitka spruce trees in blocks to the south-west, north-west and north-east of this plot and gradually, over the years, we have continued planting trees and hedges. Our vegetable garden is now protected by four hedges (of red oak, hornbeam, Lawson's cypress and privet) and blocks of spruce, larch, pine and various broad-leaved trees. To the north-east and east, additional shelter is provided by the rising land which forms a ridge known to us as the 'Bonk'.

We put up an extra inner fence. The idea was to protect our crops from rabbits and hares. But it hasn't been entirely effective—the 2-inch mesh 3-foot-high wire netting can be jumped through by baby rabbits and leaped over by adult hares—nor, I suspect, has it been entirely necessary. (We find that rabbits only take a bite here, then there, never ruining a whole crop; and hares—though perfectly capable of eating a broccoli plant to the ground—don't visit us very often.) But the fence, which in fact encompasses the hedges plus a plot of Sitka spruce and Scots pine trees as well as the vegetable garden, serves as a useful boundary mark. It is the line up to which we work when chopping back the grass, docks, nettles and willow-herb—and anything else that might drop unwanted seeds over the vegetable garden.

The gate into this garden was made by Alan twelve years ago. It is squarish and just about the right height for leaning on. It is of traditional design with diagonal braces, but—to cut costs and labour—instead of having proper mortise and tenon joints, the same effect was achieved by sandwiching 2-inch by 1-inch battens and leaving (or filling) gaps where appropriate. The whole thing is covered in wire netting and four coats of paint.

It is a good job the gate is a strong one, because it is leaned upon quite a lot. First thing in the morning we both lean upon it. Coming out of the house (breakfast cups in hand) we wander along the spring path, and stop at the entrance to the vegetable garden. We lean on the gate. What has happened overnight? Has a rabbit been in? Have any seeds germinated? The air is cool and fresh. We are distracted by little movements. Robin has seen us, and he flies from a spruce tree to sit on a fence post nearby. A spider who has been spinning all night across the top of the sage bush suddenly rushes out and gives his web a good shaking. A buzzard coasting high above the Bonk turns in a lazy circle and glides away across the top of the old rowan that stands upon our hillside. We don't speak much. We just look, and breathe, and take it all in.

In the evening Alan leans on the gate. I watch him from the kitchen window as I prepare the vegetables for dinner. His work is done for the day and he is looking at the garden. The sky behind the Carneddau is aflame with lights of gold and red. Alan puffs away at his pipe and leans there, thinking. Unless I call him in for dinner he will stay there until darkness falls and the pipistrelle bats come zippering across the garden and the blackbirds settle down noisily to roost. He turns away slowly from the garden gate, reluctant to come in.

We have a sitting place in the vegetable garden. It is at the top of the slope where there is a small 'cliff' along the line where cultivated soil ends and the wild area planted with spruce trees begins. This cliff is just a convenient height for sitting upon. Our legs dangle into the drainage ditch that we have dug along the top of the garden. We sit there mainly in the afternoons, when we have been working in the garden. One of us will straighten up and, hands pressed into creaking back, say 'I think it's time for a cup of tea.' Some of the grass along this cliff is tough and filled with nettle roots. But there is one patch where the grass is fine, soft and dense. And this is where I will find Alan sitting when I bring out the tea. (Two brimming cups, and two hunks of cake on a tray; this is going to be no ten-minute snatched rest.) With our backs amongst the thrusting branches of the spruce trees, and our bottoms upon the soft grass, we sit and look at the garden. We are warm and drowsy; the sun is full upon us. But nothing is silent. There are little movements and rustlings in the trees and grass around us. There is the hum of insects and the faint cries of sheep upon the hillside. From here we look down on the cottage. See how well the roof is looking now, *and* the chimney stack. See how much cosier it all looks since the trees have grown. We are pleased with what we see, and the tea is refreshing and the hunk of cake just what we needed after all that work. We used to be able to see the mountains from here, but since the trees have grown our view has been obscured. But in return for the loss of a distant view, we now have complete privacy. Occasionally we will hear a vehicle pass in the road, or the voices of some walkers going by. But they are nothing to do with us. That is another world out there. *This* is our world, this world of trees and grass, of delicate, trusting flowers and vigorous, strong vegetables.

I think I will go and fill the cups again . . .

We have quite a few gardening books, and in the early days we consulted them a lot. We have modern-thought compost ones—never dig deep, good mulch of compost on top; we have old-fashioned solemn ones—if you haven't dug 2 spits deep you're no gardener; we have mumbo-jumbo mystique ones—always sow when the moon is waxing; and we have 'scientific' ones—hoe in equal parts of MG.45 and Supacroppa 94 and give a dressing of LXY2.OP 21 days after sowing. The book on compost-grown vegetables is the most thumbed through; but now we know all about making compost, and have no need of a book on the subject. The old-fashioned books are interesting for occasional reference only. The mumbo-jumbo ones are a disappointment. We are now convinced that each garden has its own personal mystique; each has its own mysterious area of unaccountability, and only the gardener can discover it. There is no blanket guidance to mystery. One year we tried planting half the potatoes when the moon was waxing, and half later when it was waning. The earlier planted ones were noticeably better. The next year we reversed the procedure, and planted the first lot of potatoes when the moon was waning, and the second lot when it was waxing again. Once again, the earlier planted potatoes appeared to be better. I don't think we have opened the book since. The 'scientific' gardening books usually make Alan bad-tempered. Pages of the books are pencilled across angrily, and the word 'rubbish!' written in the margins.

Muriel is a scientific gardener. She uses a garden line to make sure her vegetables will come up in straight rows, and she always tries to do things according to the book. Alan once asked her how she calculated her spaces. Did she take the measurement from the centre of the sprout plant stalk, or its nearside or offside, or did she take into account overhang of leaves. She thought about the question for a few minutes before she realized that he was being sarcastic. However, magnanimous as always, Muriel turned the tables by presenting him with a large, scientifically produced cauliflower which he was sheepishly happy to accept. (We can't grow them at Hafod.)

Over the years we have followed quite a lot of advice from our gardening books, but now they are abandoned, gathering dust high on a kitchen shelf. This particular little vegetable plot, carved out of this particular hillside has now taught us everything we need to know. We dig, rake, sow, weed and harvest when *something* tells us to.

Hold some vegetable seeds in the palm of your hand—and you are holding a miracle. From these tiny, dormant cells of life will come next year's dinners. This miracle seems all the more astonishing when you have gathered these seeds yourself from *your* plant in *your* garden. When they have come from a packet bought from a shop, it somehow doesn't seem so miraculous. After all, it says on the packet: sow in March, and harvest in August; and things you buy in the shops are supposed to work. There are laws about it.

We would dearly love to be able to save all our own vegetable seeds, but our summers are too short for many types of seed to be able to ripen. For years we grew not very successful Brussels sprouts. In one of our gardening books it said that one of the most common causes of failure with Brussels sprouts was the use of inferior or unsuitable seed. So we tried year after year with different sorts of seed supplied by different firms. Then one year, after an unusually long and fine summer, we were able to save an abundance of seed from our own sprout plants. The years following we harvested great sprouts sometimes 2 inches in diameter, from sturdy plants. The book was right on this occasion. Once again we had proved to ourselves that home-saved seed is superior to shop seed.

The Hafod crops, grown from Hafod seed, are the crops that mean the most to us. The seeds, like us, now belong to this patch of ground. Together we live to a rhythm of sunshine and cloud, rain and wind. We respond to the feel of earth. In wintertime the cottage shelters us and our seeds whilst we wait for the coming spring. Plans are made. Throughout the winter evenings Alan will decide what shall be sown where. He makes elaborate sketch plans—changes his mind—then makes more elaborate sketches. When he eventually goes out into the garden with his spade in his hand, the plans are forgotten. The sketches are abandoned. Decisions are made by instinct, and once again the garden takes shape.

Here are the Hafod crops:

Potatoes

Surely the most important crop. Who can fear the winter when there are several hundredweight of potatoes in sacks carefully stacked in an outhouse? We try to ensure that our potato crop is lifted on a bright autumn day, with a good drying wind blowing. They come out of the ground clean and cream-coloured, and we keep them all—even the marble-sized ones. This is a time of great excitement. Alan plunges the fork in and lifts the haulm; I quickly grovel with my hands to make sure that none is lost. Sometimes, in a long, wet autumn, we have to lift them in wet conditions. They are bundled muckily into sacks and then, in turn, the sacks are emptied on to newspaper on the kitchen floor. For weeks we are edging our way around potatoes as they lie upon the floor. At all costs the crop must be saved. A large potato is almost a meal in itself. I scrub them, prick them and put them on the top shelf in the oven. After an hour they are ready—crisp, golden skins; light, feathery insides. I slice them open; drop in a knob of butter, a grating of cheese, a sprinkle of chopped chives and pepper. Food fit for the Gods!

The trouble with potatoes is that we can never grow enough of them. Alan doesn't like to grow them in the same place more than once in four years, and we haven't the time to keep on clearing fresh ground for them. Occasionally we grow them on a plateau at the top of the field within an enclosure fenced of for the purpose of growing Christmas trees. There is room enough within this area for a few plots of potatoes, and there is a reasonable depth of soil up there. But it is a long way to carry the compost. So the first time we took a spade to the turf for the purpose of planting potatoes we followed the traditional, peasants' 'lazy-bed' method of cultivation so that no nourishment was lost from the soil by removing any part of it at all. The finished lazy-bed resembles the normal potato ridge, but gets its name from the fact that the soil underneath the ridge is not dug. The first step is to turn over the sods from a furrow and place them face down, that is, grass to grass, on the ridges, so that eventually the grass rots and helps to feed the growing crop. The seed potatoes are placed on top of the upside-down sod and covered with more earth lifted from the furrow. The first year we did this we were able to top the furrows with a goodly supply of manure very kindly supplied by our neighbour Mr. Jones, who brought a trailer load and dumped it just the other side of our shared fence. From this completely exposed plot of land, at 1,050 feet above sea-level, we lifted an excellent crop of potatoes, with no wireworm or other damage. What were the varieties? Arran Pilot and Sharpes Express. We have been saving our own seed from these two ever since we came here, and they have never let us down. In a good year the Arran Pilot crop will produce potatoes so large that one is a meal for both of us. (We once weighed a particularly large Arran Pilot potato—it was 3 lb 7 oz.) Sharpes Express have an attractive, elongated-kidney shape and a delicious, nutty flavour. Both varieties keep well throughout the winter. We usually manage to grow enough Sharpes Express to last us until April and although they may be going a little soft by then, they are still good. Over the years we have tried seventeen other varieties of seed potatoes—including four French types—but they have always been a disappointment.

We select our seed potatoes by picking out good ones at the time of lifting the crop. (An ideal size is about $1\frac{1}{2}$ inches by 3 inches). We lay them out carefully in trays and keep them in the light (often out in the sun) throughout the winter. They go green, and they develop little, green, stubby leaves, and sometimes little roots as well. We turn the seed potatoes carefully throughout the winter. We plant in April, usually about the second or third week, when we can be reasonably sure that no heavy snowfalls are likely at our altitude. (Snow will be visible in pockets on the Carneddau until late June.) When planting in the garden we dig a trench, fill it with compost, make a sort of 'nest' of compost around each potato (planted about fifteen inches apart) then cover with soil, ridging it slightly. The rows are about two feet apart. Manure—if we are able to get hold of any—is spread on top.

A final note on seed potatoes. We once gave about twenty-eight pounds of rubbishy little potatoes to another neighbour, Evan Lloyd, for his pigs. It was the end of May, and these were tiny, shrivelled-up things that even *I* could not be bothered to peel. They had been hanging about in a damp bag; long shoots had grown, and most of these had been broken off. Evan didn't give them to his pigs; he tossed them, carelessly, into a furrow in one of his fields, and bunged some manure on top . . . just to see what happened, he said. What happened was a fine crop of medium to large potatoes—and this in a year which was generally not good for the crop, and certainly not good for ours at Hafod, which were a bit of a disappointment. Make what you like of this.

Kale

We wanted to be sure of a continuous supply of green food, so in the beginning we tried to grow cabbages as well as kale. We chose several varieties of savoy, all of which had to be sown at the same time but each of which, according to the claims made in the catalogue, came to maturity at a different time. In fact they all grew up together to become sad little balls (about cricket-ball size) and obviously wishing they were anywhere else but on a wind swept hill in North Wales. The kale, on the other hand, flourished.

The kale plant is not far removed from the original wild cabbage. Its reputation as a plant that will thrive on poor soil has certainly been proved at Hafod. It is so at home here that it has seeded itself quite happily all over the place, and some-times these self-set plants that appear in the paths and amongst the rough grass are better than the ones we have sown in the garden. The marvellous thing about a kale plant is that it just keeps on going. As fast as I pick the leaves, more come along. A good plant will feed us from August until the following May. This being the case, a dozen plants is really enough for us. Over

the years we have grown most varieties of kale, but our favour-
ites—from which we collect the seed—are Asparagus (large,
smooth leaves and a particularly appetizing flavour) and
Purple (a curiously notched leaf that sprouts tiny leaflets on its
top surface): this seed was originally given to us by a relative
of mine, who didn't know what its name was. So, to us, it is
now 'Uncle Bert's Purple Kale'. In a severe frost the leaves of
both these plants will droop; but they recover. The only variety
of kale we have known to stand upright and unflinching in
severe frost is Scotch Curled. But we have found this rather a
tough plant to eat (except when the leaves are very young)
and, moreover, with all those tight crinkles to investigate for
caterpillars, it is a bit of a bother to prepare.

Peas

In a good season we eat peas fresh from the plant for eleven to
twelve weeks from the end of August. Particularly large and
well-filled pods will be selected for seed . . . (We always like to
have about a pint of seed peas in stock, in case of successive
years of failure—this hasn't happened yet, but you never
know!) . . . and we also reckon to have about four pints of
dried peas in stock for eating during the winter. The peas we
intend drying for winter store will already be ageing within
their pods by the time we come to gather them. If we can pick
them all on a dry day, so much the better; but if we are unable
to do this and have to strip the plants in the rain, it doesn't
really matter because we will dry them off in the kitchen. We
spread out the pods on newspaper and leave them around the
kitchen (on the floor or on the window-ledge) turning them
every few days. When the pods begin to shrink and split open,
then is the time to shell them, and the peas can be stored in
jars. (Peas to be saved for seed are treated in a similar way.)
When cooking dried peas I soak them overnight in cold water,
simmer gently and serve as a second vegetable, or in stews, or I
make pea soup. All these peas—to eat fresh and to dry for seed
and winter stores—we get from two double 20-foot rows.

We sow our peas in early April and late May. We take out a shallow trench; fill with compost; sow the seeds about three inches apart in two staggered rows about nine inches apart, finally covering with about one and a half inches of soil. We grow the crop up netting supported on canes. (We found in the first year that twigs just snapped off in the wind. But now that the garden is sheltered—and the pea netting just about falling to pieces—we may try twigs again next year.)

Apart from the time when we allowed it to get smothered with chickweed, our pea crop has never failed us. The variety that has served us so long and faithfully is Meteor—and we can't sing its praises highly enough. The pods are always tightly packed with six to nine peas, but sometimes as many as eleven. One year we were led astray by the exhortations in a seed catalogue and we bought some seed called Everbearing. The catalogue claimed that Everbearing would produce 'a magnificent abundance of peas over an exceptionally long period'. The plants were supposed to grow to three feet, but at fifteen inches they were already loaded with tiny pea pods. Then we had to go away for a week. We left on the Sunday. When we returned the following Friday we found that every single tiny pea pod, containing about four peas, had ripened. We gathered them all in one fell swoop, and ate most of them as dried peas. Fortunately, we had also sown a row of good old Meteor which supplied us with fresh peas for the rest of the season. A final point on the excellence of our Meteor peas . . . they are allegedly a short plant, growing only to one foot. Our Meteors grow to three feet.

Broad Beans

We grow a double row of broad beans—planted in a similar fashion to the peas—but the beans are staggered so that the plants will be about nine inches apart. The row is usually about twelve feet long. The beans like it here. They grow strongly and yield well, but we have to support them before the season is over or they will blow down. (We usually put fencing posts at either end and in the middle and tie a rope around them all.) We select a dozen or so good pods for seed and these are left on the plant to ripen. We have never tried eating dried beans in winter. We are not troubled by blackfly here and before the plants get very old, we eat their leafy tops.

Jerusalem artichokes

A curious vegetable which, we have read, is not in fact an artichoke, neither does it come from Jerusalem. It is a sunflower named *Helianthus tuberosus* which was brought to England from Nova Scotia in the seventeenth century. Certainly it grows like a sunflower; ours reach 7 feet on occasions. Leastways, they *would* reach 7 feet if they remained standing. They so rarely do. Even our sheltering trees can't always stop the wind getting at the stand of artichokes. We have tried staking and tying them up, like the broad beans, but to no avail. Our Jerusalem artichoke plants usually end up in a tangled mess on the ground. But this doesn't prevent them producing tubers.

We start digging artichokes to eat in January, weather permitting. But this is also the month when artichokes are usually planted, so we now do the two jobs together. Having lifted a root, we select a good tuber for seed, and immediately go and plant it in the piece of ground we have chosen to be next year's artichoke bed. (This is usually the site of a previous compost heap, most of the compost having already been removed.) By repeatedly selecting good, even-shaped tubers for our seed we have gradually improved the shape and quality of the whole crop. Most of our artichokes are about the size of a large egg; we don't have many of the lumpy, knobbly ones that are such a nuisance to prepare for eating.

Artichokes boiled and served up like potatoes are dull. They are quite often greyish in colour and sometimes have a soapy hardness about them which is not pleasant. If they are mashed with a knob of butter after boiling, they are nice, but they are better roasted, though even then they can sometimes be hard. In our opinion there are only three ways of cooking a Jerusalem artichoke: in the chip pan, in a general stew, or as artichoke soup. Sliced or chipped and cooked in the chip pan they are absolutely delicious. With crispy outsides, and light, floury insides, they have something of a mushroomy taste. When diced and put into a stew with other vegetables they just add an additional pleasant flavour. Artichoke soup is cheap, tasty and another favourite dish of ours. Here is the recipe:

> 2 lb artichokes
> 2 or 3 onions
> 1 oz butter
> $\frac{1}{4}$ pint (approx.) milk
> cold water
> seasoning (celery salt, if you have it)
> chopped chives and parsley

Slice the onion and sauté it in a saucepan with half the butter. Do not let it brown. Add the diced artichokes and enough cold water to cover. Bring to the boil and cook until all vegetables are tender. The vegetables must now be mashed to a pulp. (I use my potato masher.) Now add the milk, seasoning to taste and chopped chives and parsley. Return to heat and bring to simmering point. Stir in the remainder of the butter just before serving.

The dish has, perhaps, one snag. It should not be served in polite company. Only the matiest of old friends should be with you after you have eaten a bowl of artichoke soup. This difficulty with the artichoke has always been recognized. A Hampshire gentleman, writing in the seventeenth century, said, 'In my judgement, which waysoever they be drest and eaten, they stir and cause a filthy loathsome sticking wind within the body.' Or, as a visiting friend put it, rather more crudely, 'I'm not eating any of those bloody fartichokes of yours!'

Garlic

Our 'scientific' gardening book considers that garlic is not worth even trying to grow in Britain, except in specially favoured parts of southern England. The paragraph is heavily pencilled across, and the word 'rubbish' written in the margin. We have been successfully growing garlic up here in the wilds for the past eleven years. We always save some for replanting and we always harvest enough to last us until the following spring. We plant it as soon as possible in the year (we have even cleared snow away in order to get the garlic in) and we usually lift it to dry off in August.

We use garlic chopped up raw in salads and sandwiches (provided we are not expecting company—and we usually aren't) and we also add it liberally to stews and soups. We have not met anyone else who uses garlic to the extent that we do. It seems to be generally accepted that garlic is 'good' for you, but people seem nervous of it, and are not quite sure what to do with it. Most people seem to have heard of the 'wipe round the salad bowl' idea, though they may never have actually done it. I have. So far as I am concerned it does nothing for the salad at all. However, it leaves me with garlic-smelling fingers so maybe it does slightly taint the bowl—which is, perhaps, all that some people require of their garlic cloves. Such whimsy is not for us, though. Garlic was meant to be *eaten*, not played about with. 'Wipe round the salad bowl' has now become a family joke to mean a perpetuated nonsense instruction that everybody quotes but nobody checks.

Shallots

Another lovable vegetable. Lovable because it is always with us; thoroughly reliable, and oh, so useful for those occasions when there are no other onions available. We eat shallots chopped up in salads, sliced up in sandwiches, grated (tricky, but possible) in stuffing, and boiled whole in stews. In a good year they will be fat and, many, and we will have shallots with us right up until shallot harvesting time again. In a bad year they may be small and few, and we have to ration our eating-shallots in order to have enough 'seed' for the following season.

We need never be without some form of onion flavour because we have the following oddities growing in various places around the garden:

Perennial spring onions

They increase by dividing. I can go and dig out a bunch any time during the spring, summer and autumn.

Welsh onions

Bulb not very useful after first year as it has a flower stem in the middle. May be used as chives. (The same applies to our *Japanese bunching onions*, *evergreen bunching onions* and various other 'fancy' onions of the 'bunching' type.)

Tree onions

Curious plants that increase by dividing, and by producing bunches of mini-onions (and sometimes seeds) on top of tall stems. Very mild flavour, useful for salads. There is a large, pithy stem in the parent bulb but it is easily removable.

The one type of onion we have never been successful in growing is the ordinary common or garden spring onion! We haven't yet been able to get hold of any potato onions to try.

Nine-star broccoli

This is a 'perennial' broccoli which produces mini-'cauliflowers' on a large plant. One year we had a nine-star broccoli that gave us thirty-nine 'cauliflower' heads during the season. Most of them were about cricket-ball size, but the main, central one was as big as a very large grapefruit. Once the last head had been taken from the plant Alan cut it back severely. The next year it gave us another good crop of heads, but the following year it produced open flowers instead of creamy curds. We let it go to seed, saved a goodly amount, and then the plant died. By sowing a small amount of seed each year we ensure that we are never without nine-star broccoli.

Spinach beet and seakale beet

Of the two vegetables, spinach beet is the tastier, but seakale beet produces larger and more abundant leaves (also thick, white, edible stems) and is more reliable. In a very dry summer the spinach beet will sometimes produce particularly small leaves and go to seed quickly (sometimes the same year as sown), whereas the seakale beet normally produces far more leaves than we can use. Once Alan had to trim from eight plants (in order to keep them in good condition) 20 gallons of unwanted leaves. These particular plants had been grown on the site of a former compost heap and had produced a multitude of massive leaves.

Purple sprouting broccoli and Brussels sprouts

The purple sprouting broccoli is a reliable, prolific plant that will produce more and more tasty shoots as fast as I pick them. But it can't compete with a hare. If a hare gets into the vegetable garden, then a plant of broccoli will be eaten to the ground overnight. Brussels sprouts we hope to be picking from the middle of December to the end of February, but we normally have to triple-stake the plants to keep them upright.

All the vegetables mentioned so far are grown year after year from home-saved seed. When saving seed from a particular plant we gather as much as we can, because we can never be sure when that particular vegetable will be able to give us seed again. In order to avoid unwanted 'crosses' we must never allow two related vegetables to go to seed in the same year. For example, one year we may leave the seakale beet and the nine-star broccoli to seed; the next year we will leave the spinach beet and purple kale; the following year the seakale beet and the asparagus kale, and so on. So, throw in a few wet summers when the seed just won't ripen and you can see why we are sometimes sowing seed that is many years old. But, if it's Hafod seed, we know it will be all right.

We once saved parsnip seed. It ripened well and looked very good, but not a single seed germinated the following year. So we rushed out and bought some shop seed. That didn't germinate either. So we had no parsnips that year. We are unable to draw any conclusions and will try to save this seed again if possible.

Other vegetables we grow regularly are: lettuces, radishes, swedes, turnips, carrots, beetroots, marrows and onions. But for these we have to buy all the seed, so we simply follow the instructions on the packet (more or less) and hope for the best. We have not had total failure with any of them, but in a cold, wet summer the results are sometimes poor. (A point worth mentioning maybe is that we have found Dobie's onion sets the most successful here. It was Dobie's onions that did so well under the massive weed cover.)

From time to time we experiment by growing previously untried vegetables. Results, as you will see from the following notes, are usually disappointing, but sometimes we get a pleasant surprise:

Winter radish (Black Spanish)

Sown late July. Good. A most useful vegetable for winter salads. Roots were tender and grew 6 to 9 inches long, and up to 2 inches in diameter.

Kohl rabi (purple and green)

Successful, but needs such a long time cooking.

Red shallots

Very poor crop.

Sweet corn

Total failure.

Tomatoes

Planted early June. Very poor. Very small fruit which failed to ripen.

Chicory

Poor, even though we put plenty of lime rubble in bed.

Scorzonera and salsify

Plants survived, but poor-sized roots; much too fiddlesome to prepare.

New Zealand spinach and orach (mountain spinach)

Failed to germinate.

Green and white sprouting broccoli

Plants did not stand up to weather.

Leeks (four varieties)

Grew to pencil size—and stayed that way for six years. Produced offsets each year, but these didn't grow either.

Runner beans and kidney beans

Plants survived, but failed to produce any beans.

Apart from peas, there is no possibility of sowing seed at intervals for a succession of crops. With the exceptions of garlic, Jerusalem artichokes and unusual vegetables, *everything* goes into the ground during April. The ground is usually much too cold and wet for it to be worthwhile making any earlier sowings, and if the job is left any later than April, then November will be breathing coldly upon us before the vegetable has gained any size.

It is perhaps the shortness of our growing season, combined with the likelihood of strong winds and heavy rain which makes the advice given in our gardening books of very limited use. Gardening books are not written for places like Hafod. Even our book for northern gardeners contains unhelpful advice like, 'Close your end cloches with a sheet of glass firmly held between stakes.' The mind boggles. *Our* winds will toss whole sheets of corrugated iron around like bus tickets. What would they do with a few cowering cloches?

On the other hand, some of the advice given in gardening books doesn't make sense wherever your garden happens to be. Take, for example, this instruction: 'Sow long varieties of beetroot in threes, with three inches between groups. Thin to two inches apart, and finally to seven inches apart.' If you can work out how that is possible, perhaps you'll let me know.

Then there is the advice upon growing winter cauliflowers to form $4\frac{1}{2}$-inch-diameter heads. This is of no practical interest to us—we can't grow them here—but it is a good example of information that doesn't bear investigation. The plot to receive your winter cauliflower plants should, we understand, be manured with cow or horse dung at 4 cwt per rod (note: 1 rod equals 16 feet 6 inches) plus sulphate of potash at $1\frac{1}{2}$ lb per rod. These manures should be applied when preparing the land for the previous crop which the cauliflowers are to follow. Early potatoes are suggested as the most suitable previous crop. Right. So we start with our early potatoes. But wait. We have to manure the ground for the potatoes the *previous autumn*. (This means we have to plan our cauliflower plot two autumns before we want to eat them.) So we apply our farmyard manure at the rate of 4 cwt per 16-foot-6-inch row, and the sulphate of potash at $1\frac{1}{2}$ lb per row, and plant our early potatoes 12–18 inches apart (i.e. seventeen to twelve potatoes per row). These potatoes are ready for lifting in August, perhaps. But what about our winter cauliflowers? In June or July we should have hoed in 3 lb of superphosphate and 3 lb of sulphate of potash and planted out our eight cauliflowers per 16-foot-6-inch row! (You might care to cost the fertilizers required for one $4\frac{1}{2}$-inch cauliflower. Or did the writer mean *square* rod? But, if this is the case, just consider . . . how many households require multiples of sixty-four cauliflowers each winter?)

Sorry if I'm harping on about these pseudo-precise gardening instructions, but they do so annoy me. How about those different sorts of peas you must sow to get your succession? This lot will mature at seventy-six days; another can be picked at seventy-eight days, a third will be ready for eating at seventy-nine days, and so on. Does *anybody* take this information seriously? At Hafod we just sow Meteor, and carry on eating peas from August until November.

Now that the seed catalogues have gone metric, the position is even worse. I wonder how Muriel copes with instructions to plant, for example, raspberries 61 centimetres apart? (And why 'up to 182 centimetres between rows'?)

Before leaving the vegetable garden let's go back and lean on the gate and have another look. I don't think I pointed out the mint bed just to the right of the central path, and the long line of raspberries that divides the garden into two main portions. See how the level of the ground has sunk since we've been cultivating this patch. Perhaps it has something to do with all the stones we have removed over the years. At the top and eastern side of the garden the grassed bank is now two feet above the soil level. Notice how the garden has been terraced down the slope so that the growing plants can look squarely up to the sky. The spinach beet is looking as good as usual; great, wide, green leaves gleaming in the sunlight. And see how strong and fat those pea pods are. The potatoes are growing lustily the other side of the raspberry row; I scraped away the soil around one of them with my fingers yesterday and pulled out a fresh young potato, oval and creamy smooth. We shall be able to start lifting them soon.

We feel a great sense of satisfaction standing here on a warm summer's evening, looking at our growing crops. This was once an open field, stony, windswept and almost barren. Now it is cosy and sheltered, thrusting with life, and offering us fresh and succulent food for the picking.

6. Fruit

'Would you like a self-fertile pear tree?' Muriel's question took us by surprise. A straightforward answer would have been to the effect that—no, we would not like a pear tree, self-fertile or otherwise. Much as we like pears, we know very well that a pear tree stands little chance of being fruitful at Hafod. But then, surely Muriel knew that too? Her garden (being nearer the Conwy Valley, and 400 feet lower than ours) contained a moderately successful plum tree, but we had never noticed any pear trees. What was she playing at? We mumbled something about the altitude at Hafod—not wanting to be too emphatic in case we hurt her feelings. She swept our excuses away, saying that she thought we liked experimenting and proving the experts wrong, and that anyway she had it tied up ready for us to take. We all went down to the bottom of her garden, and there it was. Lanky and twiggy (and not all that young), it had obviously been growing between her shed and the wall; from which position it had been forcibly removed—quite some time ago too, judging from the dried and withered roots. It was obvious that Muriel just wanted to get rid of it. (Getting rid of things was always a problem with Muriel; with a neat house and a trim garden—and not liking smoky bonfires or itinerant junk men—she was often in a dilemma. We once caught her tipping several plastic bags of lawn cuttings and an unwanted gas fire into the woods; a crime which we have never allowed her to forget.) In her bossy, organizing way, Muriel was already dragging the pear tree down to our van. As we rarely left Muriel's cottage empty handed (welcome pots of lemon curd, bags of plums and pieces of 'useful junk' for Alan were always being given to us), we decided to shrug our shoulders at this latest bounty. We tied it on to the roof rack without argument,

and crawled carefully home with the windscreen partially
obscured by the mud-encrusted tangle of roots.

We planted it in a comparatively sheltered corner of the
wych-elm plot, gave it our blessing and a bucket of compost,
then forgot about it. If pear trees have karmas, then this one
was doomed from birth. To start life in a crack between Muriel's
shed and the wall, and to end it up here on the moors is a fate
that no pear tree would choose. No matter how optimistically
self-fertile, the odds were against it. Our pear tree has survived.
Just. Each year it produces a few hopeful white blossoms; and
each year a little more of it dies at the top. Alan prunes the
dead bits off each year, and the pear tree is getting shorter and
shorter. One day it will disappear.

It must be nice to pick pears from a tree in your garden;
even nicer if you can also help yourself to plums and apples.
But we accepted, from the start, that these delights would not
be ours at Hafod. However, this didn't mean that we had to be
without fruit, and—as soon as we could—we were growing
soft fruits in every corner possible.

We started with strawberries and raspberries. Wild varieties
of both fruits were growing on the roadside bank and in the
hedge, so we saw no reason why we shouldn't make a success of
cultivated ones in the garden. We had brought half a dozen
eight-year-old Royal Sovereign strawberry plants with us from
Bristol (from Alan's mother's garden) and we planted them out
on a slope in the front garden. They flourished, and produced
quite a few runners, so we started to make a proper bed of
them. More runners were taken into the bed each year, until
our final strawberry plot measured about five feet by eight
feet. During the strawberry season this little bed gave us a small
bowlful of fruit to eat fresh daily for about three weeks, and
enough strawberries to make two or three pounds of delicious jam plus a few pounds preserved by bottling. Unfortunately the 1976 drought devastated our strawberry bed.
However, even then, a few sturdy runners were found the
following year, lurking in the grass paths alongside the old bed.
One of these runners has since grown into a strong plant (which

gave us a handful of strawberries this year) so perhaps we can start again. This means that we have been growing strawberries from the same stock for thirteen years in the same bed without encountering any serious troubles—until the drought came.

To keep the fruits off the ground we use wheat straw, wood straw, wood shavings, paper shavings or coconut fibres—all of which do the job quite adequately. The birds (especially the blackbirds and mistle thrushes) are as fond of strawberries as we are, so we try to preserve some for ourselves by 'netting' the bed. We push sticks (about 18 inches long) into the ground at 2-foot intervals, invert jam jars on to the sticks, cover all with ¾-inch netting, and place stones and bricks around the edges to hold down the net. Even so, the first job of the day during the season is going out to see who's caught up in the strawberry bed.

The raspberries—after an initial false start—have never let us down. We made a mistake in the beginning by planting some canes near the spring. (We were obviously over-reacting to advice in our gardening books which said that raspberries needed plenty of moisture.) These plants became weedy, feeble and produced no flowers. So we planted a row in the vegetable garden, and their healthy, vigorous growth proved that this was the right place for them. We now have a 30-foot line of raspberries straight up the middle of the garden. The plants are on an 18-inch-high bank which often seems to get completely dried out in the spring and summer, yet we normally have excellent crops of juicy, thimble-sized raspberries. On some days at the time of the August glut I can be picking as much as eight pounds of raspberries at once. During a good season we hope to gather a total of forty to fifty pounds. The variety? Lloyd George. The plants we brought with us from Bristol, from stock that was originally planted in Alan's mother's garden in 1929.

We have to protect the canes from the wind and the berries from the birds and, in order to facilitate netting the crop, Alan is constantly pruning the canes. No fruiting shoots are allowed to extend more than 9 inches out of the line, and all canes are 'tipped' at 2 foot 6 inches. During the year all new

canes which are out of line, or too thin or too crowded, are removed. This pruning work is halted during the height of the
picking season when many unwanted canes are inaccessible,
but as soon as the crop is finished, all the old canes and most of
the new ones are removed, at or below ground level. So,
during autumn, winter and spring there will be a single row
of canes, 4 or 5 inches apart, about 2 feet 6 inches high, all
woven into and tied to a 'fence' of four strands of wire.

Pruning is *his* work. Netting the bushes, disentangling caught
birds, picking, sorting, cleaning, bottling, jamming, making
tarts and pies, is *her* work. The only part of this 'treadmill' that
I find a laborious chore is the sorting and cleaning. Some of the
raspberries may have been visited by flies. But if I find a large,
succulent raspberry with a maggoty bit on one side I can
neither discard it, nor ignore it. I pinch out the bad bit and re-
tain the good bit. Going through eight pounds of raspberries in
this way (knowing that I can't leave the job, because there may
be another eight pounds tomorrow) is a wearisome task if I am
obliged to do it indoors on a dull, wet day and I am huddled at
the sink and keep on having to wipe my fingers on a cloth. If it is
warm and bright, and I am sitting at the spring, it's a different
matter. Then I don't mind how long the job takes. All other
work is cheerfully abandoned. I'll sit here all day in the sun
picking over the raspberries, dibbling my fingers in the water
when necessary, and flicking all the bad bits anywhere I like
(much to Alan's annoyance because he keeps having to remove
tiny raspberry seedlings from the ground all around every
sitting place in the garden). During August the raspberry crop
keeps me busy every day. In the meantime, other fruit is fast
ripening.

Blackcurrants have never been an outstanding success with
us but, because we have so many bushes dotted about the place,
we usually manage to pick five to ten pounds each year. (We
have five varieties, but Mendip Cross is by far the best.) On
this poor, thin, stony soil the bushes haven't much to sustain
them, and we can rarely afford to give them any compost.
When we first planted them we followed the advice in a garden-

ing book and pruned them to about eight inches above the ground. The bushes developed no new growth and we had no fruit from them the next year. So—following the book once more—we pruned them again, this time to 4 inches. Again, no new growth. So we just left them alone and we found, after a couple of years, that the bushes threw out a little new growth from the old wood, and these new bits fruited. Eventually we were able to take cuttings from the original plants and now these cuttings have developed into medium-sized bushes (which we never prune) and they supply us with fruit every year. Once again, we have to protect this fruit from the birds— with netting, lace curtains, and anything else that comes to hand. (A large net petticoat of mine, left over from the 1950s when such things were in fashion, made an ideal cover for one bush.)

The least bothersome and most reliable cultivated Hafod fruit is the gooseberry. Good old faithful gooseberries, getting on with the job of growing and swelling and not being at all demanding of attention whilst I rush around snatching at strawberries, raspberries and blackcurrants before the birds get them. Gooseberries have to be really ripe and dropping off the bush before the birds take much notice of them—by which time *I* am usually ready to deal with the fruit.

We started off with half a dozen plants of Careless goose-berry, ordered by post. They were miserable, weedy little things, and looked exactly like a sketch drawn in one of our gardening books, a sketch labelled 'an example of a rubbishy four-year-old gooseberry plant'. The following year these bushes produced so much fruit the tiny branches were in danger of snapping under the weight. Each year Alan has care-fully pruned them, fed them with wood ash, and generally cosseted them. Now, ten years later, they look like 'rubbishy five-year-olds'—and they still produce a great quantity of fruit whatever the weather. We have taken successful cuttings from these plants, and we also have some minute seedling bushes sprouting up perkily from the ground beneath the parent plants—presumably from ripened gooseberries that

dropped and lay unnoticed. We have also increased our stock
of gooseberry bushes by adding to them varieties reputed to be:
Golden Drop, Whinhams Industry, Leveller, Lancashire Lad
and Warrington. The implied doubt here is intentional. None
of these latterly purchased bushes has the habit of growth or
colour of fruit that it is supposed to have. All we can say is that
they reward us each year with a good crop of green or red
gooseberries, but none is quite so prolific as the Careless
variety. When pruning the bushes Alan tries to maintain a neat,
inverted open-umbrella shape. This is in order to let the sun
reach all parts of the plant, and for ease of fruit picking. His
care of the bushes seems to work. We pick fifty to seventy
pounds of gooseberries each year. We eat gooseberries straight
from the bush as we wander around; we eat them chopped up
in salads; we have them in pies and tarts, or stewed (with a
sprig of elderflower). I preserve dozens of bottles of them; I
make pounds of jam with them and—if they are still falling from
the bushes—I make gooseberry chutney. Here is the recipe for
the last lot of gooseberry chutney that I made. (The proportions of gooseberries, onions, sugar and vinegar are consistent
each time I make it, but not necessarily the dried fruit and
spices. If I haven't raisins, I use sultanas or currants. The dates
and apple are sometimes left out altogether. The spices are to
the quantities that we like, but these can be varied as you wish.)

GOOSEBERRY CHUTNEY

3 lb gooseberries
$\frac{1}{2}$ lb onions
$\frac{1}{2}$ lb raisins
6 oz dates
1 apple
$\frac{1}{2}$ teaspoonful mixed spice powder
$\frac{1}{4}$ teaspoonful ground ginger
$\frac{1}{4}$ teaspoonful cayenne pepper
$\frac{1}{2}$ teaspoonful peppercorns
4 cloves   } all tied in a
2 pieces root ginger   } muslin bag

3 teaspoonsful mixed spice berries ⎫ all tied in a
3 chillies   ⎬ muslin bag
1 pint vinegar   ⎭
1 lb sugar (preferably brown)

Top and tail the gooseberries, peel onions, peel and core the apple, clean the dried fruit if necessary—I usually find that it is—and put the lot through the mincer (coarse cutter). (This instruction to mince the fruit and onion will probably make chutney purists shudder. If you prefer a chunky chutney, then by all means chop up these ingredients with a knife.) Put all the ingredients *except the sugar* into your preserving pan, or very large saucepan. Cook very slowly until all the ingredients are tender and the vinegar is much reduced. (This can take up to 4 hours.) Now remove the bag of spices. Add the sugar and stir thoroughly until dissolved. The cooking must now be speeded up; keep stirring to make sure the mixture is not sticking to the bottom of the pan. The chutney is ready when it has lost that 'watery' look. Spoon it into hot jars and cover at once.

Following on with our idea of growing in the garden cultivated varieties of the fruit which is flourishing in the hedgerow, we have planted around the vegetable garden fence three varieties of blackberry: Himalayan Giant, Bedford Giant and Merton Thornless. These plants soon settled down at Hafod and are now growing lustily, sending out in all directions strong branches which are laden with fruit. The berries are large and juicy—some of the berries on the Himalayan Giant reaching pigeon's egg size. There is, however, one snag. The fruit on all three varieties is absolutely tasteless. Fruit from these bushes is only tolerable, in a pie for example, if mixed with wild blackberries. So, on the whole, we have by-passed the cultivated ones and concentrated upon harvesting the abundance of delicious blackberries growing in our hawthorn hedges. We seem to have at least four different varieties of wild ones, including a particularly shiny blackberry that tangles happily between the road and our bottom pond and has a habit of growth like a raspberry. In the meantime, however, the cultivated, tasteless aliens have been taking over the vegetable garden fence, which is in danger of being flattened beneath the weight of all that sturdy growth and those great insipid berries. The Himalayan Giant was being a particular nuisance, so we decided to get rid of it. After all, this was ridiculous; even the birds didn't seem to want the fruit. So Alan hacked it down, dug up the root and transplanted it into a corner of the wych-elm plot where we decided it could do what it liked without bothering us. Once again, it settled down, put out roots and branches everywhere, and proceeded to take over the entire corner. But if we thought that we had things under control, we were mistaken. Alan must have left a bit of root behind, because last year we noticed great sturdy shoots thrusting up alongside the fence once more, and those depressingly healthy branches are reaching out to grab at anything handy. So now we have *two* tasteless Himalayan Giants threatening to engulf us.

Another sturdy embarrassment that we wish we'd never thought of in the first place is the loganberry. We bought three plants originally, one of which was a thornless variety. We've been moving them around the garden ever since—not because the fruit they bear is tasteless, but because it is practically non-existent. Amongst a thicket of healthy branches I will be lucky to find three or four loganberries. When moving the loganberry bushes we ran into the same difficulty as with the blackberry. We have never managed to get all the roots out, and useless loganberry plants are pushing up through the soil all around the place.

Japanese wineberry. Now here is an attractive and trouble-free little fruit bush. It has growing habits similar to the blackberry, but it is a much daintier plant, with pretty red hairs up the stem and over the fruit buds. The fruit is like a small raspberry, but it is very slightly sticky to touch and, possibly because of this stickiness, it is left severely alone by both birds and insects. It is not so tasty as a raspberry, but none the less enjoyable in a pie. It needs to be grown up a fence, and tied to it, because—unlike the blackberry—it is somewhat fragile and the branches can be snapped off in the wind. We planted a Japanese wineberry in a corner of the vegetable garden against the fence. It has been very well behaved, but it has not grown much. It puts up only one shoot each year. At the moment we pick enough fruit from it each autumn to fill about one small pudding basin. One year, the berries ripened whilst we were away, and there must have been some strong winds in our absence. The plant was still tied to the fence, but all the little berries had blown on to the ground.

We have four redcurrant bushes. When we ordered these bushes we requested two redcurrant bushes and one white-currant and—according to the labels that accompanied them—this is what we received. But when the bushes came to bearing fruit it was obvious that we had three redcurrant bushes, by which time the delivery note had been lost. Was it worth while having an argument with the supplier? We decided that it was. We sent a letter of complaint and, within a week, we received another plant which we were assured was the variety White Versailles. The nursery apologized and blamed their new computer for the error. The following year this plant bore a fair crop of *red* berries. So we shrugged our shoulders. What's more, we have been shrugging our shoulders at these bushes ever since because although all four are laden with fruit each year, we are lucky if we can gather a single bowlful of it. As a whisky bottle is to an alcoholic, so a redcurrant bush is to a blackbird, and at redcurrant-picking time we are usually supporting two families of drunken blackbirds who seem to spend their days calculating devious ways of getting past the barriers into the redcurrant bushes. They will take the odd peck at the blackcurrants if given a chance, and they certainly won't walk straight past the raspberries or strawberries either, but if these are well protected, the assaults are a bit half-hearted. But not so with the redcurrants. The blackbirds consider that these are theirs by some divine right, and they are most affronted when we rudely interrupt their feasting. A blackbird discovered in the redcurrant bushes will do anything to avoid leaving them.

He will flop through the bush to the other side; he will drop to the ground and run round to another bush. If you actually catch him and physically remove him he will fly to the nearest hedge and sit there swearing loudly. You may replace the netting and weight it down with bricks, stones or logs, but as soon as your back is turned, blackbird will be back in amongst the redcurrants again.

Rhubarb we don't take too seriously, but we wouldn't like to be without it. We brought a root with us from Bristol (Alan's mother's garden again) which formed the basis of our main bed, but we have also grown some more from seed. We bought several varieties of rhubarb seed and sowed them out of doors, in accordance with the instructions on the packet. There was good germination, and some healthy little seedlings sprouted up. The best were planted out; they flourished and we were pulling sticks of rhubarb to eat the first year. (This was not recommended on the packet, but as the leaves were big enough to flap about in the wind and we could see they were going to get broken off anyway, we decided we might as well pull them.) Two of these rhubarbs grown from seed are very red-stemmed varieties and the Timperley Early is a particularly attractive and tasty one. We now have several beds dotted around the garden, and we find that the plants can grow in rough grass and cope quite well. We tear away the grass and give these beds of rhubarb some compost occasionally, but otherwise we leave them alone. I think it's good to have an abundance of rhubarb because it is ready to eat before the earliest fruits of the year, and the making of the first rhubarb tart in the springtime is one of the signals that the season of plenty is on the way. It is also available late in the year. When the last of the berries have been taken from the bushes and autumn is nudging closer, the question of 'what shall we have for pudding?' can often be answered by wandering out into the garden and finding a rhubarb bed. Having been left alone all summer, whilst I've been fussing with the serious matter of fruit-gathering, the humble rhubarb patch can now offer a second helping of red sticks, and stewed rhubarb, or rhubarb tart appears once more on the table. I very rarely bottle any rhubarb, and I have never made jam with it.

Jam-making is a regular summer activity of mine, but my first attempt (when newly married) was a complete disaster. I blame my recipe book. Alan blames me. I followed the instructions implicitly. Alan claims that anyone who follows obviously suspect instructions without question is an idiot.

My jam book contains many useful recipes and I use it quite a lot. It gives all sorts of ideas and information and is a thoroughly excellent book in all respects except one. It contains the instruction: 'When sugar has dissolved, boil jam RAPIDLY WITHOUT STIRRING.' Note the capital letters. They jump out of the book at you. I was making blackberry jam, and I was boiling it RAPIDLY WITHOUT STIRRING. I was not happy. I was itching to plunge in my wooden spoon to test what was happening on the bottom of the pan, but I was intimidated by those capital letters. Alan came into the kitchen, sniffing.

Alan: 'Is that jam all right?'

Me: 'I think so.'

Alan: 'Are you sure it's not burning?'

Me: 'I hope not.'

Alan: (peering into the pan, and then looking around for the spoon) 'Why don't you give it a stir?'

Me: 'Because it says not to.'

Alan: 'Why not?'

Me: 'I don't know. It doesn't say.'

Alan: (shrugging) 'Well, don't ask me to clean the pan if it is.'

It was. And I didn't. But he did.

Alan will always rise to an emergency, and that pan was an emergency. The bottom quarter inch was adhesive-reinforced-blackberry-charcoal-concrete. The next half inch was glutinous-semi-set-reinforced-blackberry-concrete, and the rest looked, and smelt, like lumpy-burnt-black-treacle.

Since then I stir my jam frequently . . . and I have never had a failure.

Other people's failures don't seem to be so dramatic as mine.

I understand that jam failing to set, and jam going mouldy in store are the two most common problems. I have theories about both of them. I think that if jam fails to set, then it just hasn't been boiled long enough (always assuming that correct proportions of sugar and, if necessary, lemon juice have been added). The traditional ways of testing if a jam is set are (1) dropping a bit on a saucer and if it wrinkles when pushed it is set, and (2) with a thermometer. I have tried the first one, and I think it is too vague. I can't comment on the use of a sugar thermometer because I have never had one, but surely it's all a matter of evaporation of water from the boiling jam? When the boiling jam loses that 'sloppy' appearance, and starts dragging on the spoon in a thick and tacky sort of way—then it's done! As for the jam going mouldy, this cannot happen if the jam is put, whilst still hot, into absolutely clean and sterile jars which are immediately sealed with sterile lids. I obtain complete sterility by washing jars, then rinsing them in cold water, then, *without wiping them with a tea towel*, placing them on a thick metal tray and putting them first in the bottom (slow) oven, then transferring the tray to the top (hot) oven. (Often when I fill my hot jars with hot jam, the jam boils again inside the jars.) If I am using jars that have screw-top lids, the lids will have been dunked in boiling water before being slapped on the jars (using tongs to handle them). If I am using jam jars that are traditionally covered with cellophane circles and rubber bands, I do *not* use the little wax circles that you are supposed to drop on to the jam surface. There is no way of making these sterile, and it's asking for trouble to use them.

We eat our way through many pounds of jam each year—in puddings, tarts and piled on to hunks of bread and butter. We enjoy it, but we wonder if there can be much food value (other than calorific) in jam; with all that sugar and all that boiling, we are doubtful.

Sometimes I make rose-hip syrup, which is allegedly full of vitamin C, and we like to have it on rice puddings and semolina puddings during the winter. Here is my recipe:

ROSE-HIP SYRUP
2 lb ripe rose-hips
1 lb white sugar
3 pints water

Mince the rose-hips and drop them into a saucepan containing 2 pints of boiling water. Bring to the boil quickly, then remove the saucepan from the heat and leave 15 minutes. Pour through a jelly-bag, and allow to drip overnight. Return the pulp to the saucepan, add a pint of boiling water, bring to the boil again, and then allow to stand (without further heating) for another 10 minutes, then drain through the jelly-bag as before (but not necessarily leaving it overnight). Combine the two lots of juice in the preserving pan (or a very large saucepan) and simmer until it is reduced to approximately $1\frac{1}{2}$ pints. (It is better to use a preserving pan because the evaporation of liquid will be quicker.) Add the sugar and boil again for a further 5 minutes. Pour the hot syrup into sterile jars and seal immediately with sterile lids as described for jam-making. (If you have suitable bottles and corks—and the means of sterilizing them—you may find that this is a handier way of storing the syrup.)

We start the winter with shelves lined with row after row of gleaming jars of bottled fruit, jams, syrup and chutney. It all represents a lot of work . . . but oh, what satisfaction it brings! I often go and peer at them all, and gloat. It almost seems a shame to open them!

7. Herbs

I am unable to define a *herb*. I have one dictionary which claims that a herb is a plant with no woody stem above ground (what about sage?), and another dictionary gives the definition: 'a plant producing shoots of only annual duration' (what about rosemary?). Most people accept that a herb is an aromatic culinary plant (what about comfrey?), and a book of herbal cures I was reading the other day was on about oak trees. I give up. I am simply going to tell you about the herbs at Hafod.

The front garden is a triangular patch of land with hawthorn hedges on two sides, and the house, shippen and pigsty on the third side. The land is sloping and terraced, with grass paths and small flights of stone steps connecting the terraces. There is a strawberry bed here; also beds of gooseberries, black-currants and redcurrants. The pathways are bordered with parsley, wild thyme, common thyme and thymes of lemon, orange and caraway fragrance. At the bottom of the terraces a broad grass path leads alongside the hawthorn hedge from the pigsty to the front gate. At the base of the hawthorn hedge grow plants of comfrey, horse-radish and sweet rocket. At the top of the terraces a winding grass path leads from the front door of the house to the front gate. This path curves between mixed hedges of hazel, rose, laburnum, privet, beech, snow-berry and flowering currant. Here a marjoram plant tangles at the base of the rose hedging, and there—on the corner—the southernwood grows alongside the rosemary. Lavender bushes edge the path and sage plants peep from behind them.

On this path at the top of the terrace we have a sitting place. The bank behind us is topped with a hawthorn hedge, and behind the hedge is the wild plot of ground where the wych-elm stands. We sit here on summer afternoons when the garden is

flooded with warmth and scent. There are little close-at-hand
sounds, like the rustle of a vole on the bank, the croak of a frog
in the sage bushes, or the whirr of insect wings; and there are
far-away sounds like the call of a sheep on the hill, or the cry of
a buzzard overhead. There are staccato sounds, like the scold-
ing of a wren in the hedge; and there are dreamy sounds, like
the slow murmur of the wind in the wych-elm boughs.

We are never quite sure which way to look. With our backs
to the bank, the sun is full and warm upon our faces and we
can look out over the front hedge to the distant hills. But there
are little noises from the bank behind us and we want to turn
around. We move slowly, because there may be a lizard snoozing upon a sun-warmed stone, or a bank vole trundling along
its grassy run carrying food home for the family. One of us will
notice a peacock butterfly dancing over the lavender spikes,
and—look—beneath the tree of heaven in the warm dust, a
young blackbird is sunbathing, with wings and tail feathers
spread out in awkward angles of ecstasy. There is so much to
see and smell and feel and listen to, our senses are bemused
with delight.

It wasn't always like this.

When we came here in 1965 the triangular patch enclosed
by the farm buildings and the hawthorn hedges was a sunken
hollow filled with grass, docks and nettles which humped and
dipped every now and then in a way that was somehow sug-
gestive of unmentionable objects buried beneath. Four doors
open out on to this area of land: the pigsty door, the shippen
door, the outhouse door and the cottage door, and it became
obvious, as we started to clear away the vegetation, that objects had been hurled into this patch from all four doors for the
past hundred years or so. We removed kettles, horseshoes, ink
bottles, a bicycle oil lamp, broken china and glass, pieces of
harness, old physic bottles, modern motor cycle bits, plastic
buckets, broken parts of old implements, and the skeleton of
a cow. But we realized, as the ground became clearer, that all
those years of mucking out the pigsty and shippen into this
triangle had presented us with a bonus. We found, in patches,

that we were digging into pure manure. As this front garden
was also a bit of a sun trap, and sheltered from the wind, we
decided to make it into a place for growing special things. We
didn't *have* any special things to begin with, so we grew kale
and peas and other vegetable crops as the ground was gradually
cleared and shaped. Eventually it became our main herb and
fruit garden.

We started off with garden sage and thyme, which we grew
from seed and planted out along a terraced bank. It settled
down happily. It obviously liked it upon this bank, and the
plants grew and flourished. We grew lavender from seed and
planted this in between the sage bushes. The lavender and sage
grew together in a continuous hedge at the top of the bank,
and the thyme bushes mingled to form a smaller hedge lining
the base of the bank. We grew more and different thymes—
some with fancy leaves, others with fancy flowers and many
with various pungent scents. They cushion the stones of the
steps and sometimes wander into the grass paths. We keep the
bushes neatly clipped, and in high summer the bankside is
alight with shades of palest mauve and deepest purple. Peacock
butterflies, tortoise-shells and red admirals dance all day
around the bank, and the bees cling drunkenly to the sage
flowers and bumble amongst the thyme blossom. For several
days one summer the sage bushes were visited by a pair of
humming-bird hawk moths. We stared in fascination as they
hovered in front of the flowers, their long tongues gently
probing each blossom.

Our herb garden grew. We planted sweet marjoram, pot
marjoram and wild marjoram. We grew rosemary, southernwood, sweet basil and cotton lavender. We sowed the seeds of
pot marigolds, winter savory, summer savory, rue, caraway,
angelica and coriander. We planted lilies of the valley, bugle,
clary and self-heal.

The rubbish tip was becoming a wonderland.

We set out a spearmint bed, and regretted it. It romped
through the lilies, across the path and into the poppies. So we
imprisoned it between four slabs of slate. Mint doesn't like

being imprisoned. After a couple of years it was looking sad, and begging to be let out. So we moved it to a small patch of ground we had cleared in between the main rhubarb patch and the vegetable garden fence. Here the spearmint is happy. It dances up to the vegetable garden fence and pokes impudent fingers through. It challenges the rhubarb; it sneaks across the path to the elder shrubbery and is even peeping out the other side now. We brought other mints to join it: horse mint, round-leaved mint, peppermint, and eau-de-Cologne mint. They jostle and hug each other in a glorious mint jungle. We shall chop off their noses if they push too far through the vegetable garden fence, but otherwise they can go where they like.

The chives are planted out in clumps alongside other paths. Alan cuts them back and divides them when necessary.

Another plant that thrives with an occasional severe chop is the comfrey. We have many roots of comfrey growing at Hafod, alongside the stream as well as in the front garden. Most of them came from an original plant that I brought home in my saddlebag, having dug the comfrey up from the roadside bank on my way home from Llanrwst one day. I had often noticed this large patch of comfrey growing across the field, into the hedge, down the bankside and along the road verge, and being well aware of the local council's poison spray policy, I had no guilty conscience about digging up a bit of root. We knew the comfrey as an attractive wild flower and, having also read of its outstanding nutritional qualities,* I decided that this was something we should be growing at Hafod. All those massive leaves, tasting faintly of cucumber, would make a welcome addition to our green salads. It is a boisterous plant, producing an abundance of leaves, and I had read that at one time farmers used to plant it in their fields for the nourishment of their cattle. There was a large patch rollicking away in the field be-

* I have also read recently about the allegedly 'high alkaloid content' of comfrey. Alkaloids, I gather, are not good for you—and the arguments for and against this plant are still raging. However, the 'comfrey crisis' leaves us unmoved. We have been eating young leaves of comfrey in season for about ten years with no apparent ill effect, and we see no reason to stop now even if it does mean a few extra alkaloids in our salad.

hind the hedge and I presumed that such was the case here. It was therefore with some embarrassment that, when I straightened up, I came eye to eye with a person whom I took to be the farmer staring at me from across the top of the hedge. I felt that some explanation was called for.

Me: (feeling uncomfortable) 'Oh, I'm helping myself to a bit of comfrey.'

Farmer: 'Eh?'

Me: (brightly) 'I expect all this out here came from your field didn't it?'

Farmer: 'Eh?'

Me: (I tend to jabber on and on when I'm embarrassed) 'It's very good for the cattle isn't it. Did *you* plant the field with it, or was it your predecessor?'

Farmer: 'Eh?'

Sensing that we weren't getting anywhere with this dialogue, I cut it short by wishing him a cheerful good morning, stuffing the comfrey into my saddlebag, and pedalling off.

Many of our herbs delight us all the year round. We have their taste and fragrance with us in winter as well as summer, because I always dry a large quantity. I pick bunches of lavender and southernwood and scatter them amongst our bed linen and woollies. Our pillows and sheets are lavender scented and, with any luck, the southernwood is keeping the moths from our woollen clothes.

We eat sage, marjoram, thyme and parsley almost daily. In summertime we take these herbs fresh from the plant to have chopped in our salads, in sandwiches, stews, stuffing and omelettes. I pick bunches of sage, marjoram and thyme to dry for winter use; parsley can be freshly picked from the garden all year round except in prolonged severe winter weather. We don't eat rosemary, but I always like to put a sprig of it upon a joint of lamb when cooking. The aroma of rosemary-scented lamb sizzling in the oven is mouth-watering. We now think that lamb cooked without it is relatively tasteless.

We eat a lot of all the mints (except the eau-de-Cologne). Freshly chopped spearmint, peppermint and watermint add a refreshing 'bite' to a green salad, and I always dry large bunches of spearmint for use in winter as mint sauce.

When picking herbs to dry for winter I choose a sunny day (preferably not too hot and with a light wind moving) and tie them in small bunches along my clothes line. I leave them there all day. Ideally, all herbs should be gathered for drying just before the plant comes into bloom, as the leaves are then at their most pungent. I bring in the bunches at the end of the day; tie loosely woven cloth around them (butter muslin or cheesecloth is ideal, but I have found nylon and terylene quite satisfactory), then I hang them in the kitchen to dry off completely. It is essential not to have the bunches too dense or packed tight as the inner sprigs may go mouldy if they don't dry off quickly enough. I leave my herbs like this—wrapped in their separate bunches—all winter, and I take leaves from them as I want them. It may be tidier to remove all the leaves when they are dry and crush them into small, neatly labelled jars, but as soon as you crumble an aromatic leaf you are losing some of its pungency. I prefer my herbs to be tasty—and will put up with them being untidy. This is particularly true of spearmint. I have tried other ways of preserving mint for use in winter— actually making up the mint sauce and sealing in jars, or making a mint jelly—but I have found that by far the most effective way of saving mint is simply to dry it. When mint sauce is required, simply strip off some dried leaves and crumble them between your fingers into the vinegar. The mint leaves look brownish and unattractively shrivelled when dried, but as soon as you start to crumble the leaves, that marvellous fragrance of mint is released, and when the crumbled mint meets the vinegar it seems to be rejuvenated and you will find that the appearance of the final mint sauce is perfectly acceptable.

Not all the herbs we planted or sowed have survived. We tried to grow wormwood, without success, and the winter savory, angelica and caraway seem to have died out. But the herbs we use most of—sage, thyme, marjoram, rosemary, parsley and mint—have flourished. The thymes and parsley are particularly abundant. They are now seeding themselves happily all over the place and I don't have to wander far from the back door or the front door to be able to pick a sprig of either plant.

In order to encourage the growth of our plants we have, over the years, experimented with 'sympathetic planting'. This concerns the belief that certain plants will affect certain other plants in a beneficial or adverse way, and it therefore behoves the sympathetic gardener to make sure that each plant has a happy bedfellow. (I don't mean the sheer physical presence of another plant making life uncomfortable for its neighbour, by overshadowing or crowding out, but an intangible unhappiness that crops up between the plants. After all, you can—without any apparent reason—instinctively dislike someone with whom, say, you have to share a railway carriage, and there is no evidence to prove that a plant cannot have a similar instinct.) Whilst completely accepting the concept that plants will and do affect each other, we have now come to the conclusion that no sweeping generalizations can be made. We believe that certain *individual* plants may disagree with other *individual* plants, but that their hostility is not necessarily shared by other plants of the same species. It is up to each gardener to discover for himself the feelings of his plants, and to take action accordingly.

Before we had worked this out for ourselves we were taking the advice given in books about sympathetic planting. But we found that the experts didn't agree with each other, and sometimes even contradicted themselves. Having read that rue could not live with sage and that if you put the two together one of them would die, Alan hastily moved our rue plant that he had put amongst the sage bushes. The rue survived the move, but two of the fancy sage bushes died. A couple of years later he read another book by the same author in which the tale was told of the monks in olden days who used to plant rue in with their sage bushes in order to protect them. By this time the transplanted rue had died anyway but—surprise, surprise—a rue seedling was now gallantly growing amongst the sage bushes close to the spot where the original rue had grown. We now take our instructions from plants, not from books, and we don't think there is any ill will in the garden.

About the same time we were also following herbal advice on millipedes in our potato bed, and eelworm amongst the daffodil bulbs. Neither pest was very troublesome but, having read that two species of Mexican marigold (*Tagetes erecta* and *Tagetes patula*) would destroy these pests, we decided to experiment. After a lot of difficulty we finally found a supplier of the two varieties of marigold seed. We prepared a seed box in the kitchen and carefully looked after the seedlings when they appeared. We planted them out amongst the potatoes and the daffodils and they bloomed prettily all summer. The potatoes didn't look any happier than before; the crop we lifted was about the same and there appeared to be just as many millipedes in the soil. Our eelworm wasn't eradicated either; the following spring we found a few daffodil plants still obviously affected by it. The marigolds didn't seed themselves, and we haven't seen them since.

We have several books on herbs. They give descriptions of the plant, cultural instructions, historic information, and culinary and medicinal uses. At one time we consulted them a lot, but now that we know more about our herbs, these books have been slightly demoted. They are used less as reference books, and more as entertainment.

We have tried herbal cures on two occasions. I once tried to remove a small cyst by the prolonged and patient use of cleavers (*Galium aparine*). Alan once tried to cure eczema with blackberry and elder leaves. Neither 'cure' worked. We would certainly not dismiss all herbal cures as a result of these two failures. Perhaps it is a case of finding the right herb for the right person; each of us may respond differently to different herbs. But I must confess that the ambiguous waffle that one reads in some herb books and so-called nature-cure magazines is a bit off-putting. It's nice to know that the parsley I'm chewing will protect me against 'general weakness and tired blood', and that thyme is excellent if my kidneys are 'deranged' or my mind 'disordered', but I do wish we could have more details of the 'life-giving powers' and 'healthful properties' that so many books quote. Have you ever noticed the large number of herbal cures there are for 'female ailments'? If you have uterine disorders, delayed menstruation, difficulty in labour, a delay in the appearance of your afterbirth, or you wish your flow of milk to be improved . . . there's a herb growing somewhere for you! This 'female' element in itself sets me wondering. Is it because, traditionally, the people who dished out these cures were old women of the woods? Or were most of their customers women? Or is it only us damn-fool women who believe in all this nonsense? I don't know. Alan and I are so rarely ill that we have not had occasion to try any herbal cures, other than the two I mentioned, so we are not in a position either to condemn or recommend herbal medicines. But herbs form part of our daily diet; is this why we remain healthy?

However, there is one area of mystic healing that I think is worth investigating; this is the cult of 'flower exultation'. A book I have been reading on the subject claims that having a melancholy heart and a spirit that is low and depressed will expose a person to all the ills of mankind from heart disease to varicose veins. Cure the depression and melancholy and you are well on the way to being cured of everything else. Those despondent and despairing thoughts can be driven away, it is claimed, by 'flower exultation', that is, drinking water that has received 'beneficial powers' from certain flowers. The water will receive these powers if the blossom head is held over the water, provided you are in communication with the flower and are thinking appropriate thoughts. The book gives instructions for gathering your own flower power, and lists an appropriate do-it-yourself kit. To begin with, it is essential to get up early on a midsummer morning when it is sunny, and approach your chosen group of flowers, asking their permission to take power from them. You must have with you a bottle of spring water and a cut-glass bowl, plus *half a bottle of brandy*, which is necessary to preserve the agent of healing once it has been received by the water.

I am now a disciple of flower exultation. Next midsummer I shall go and sit amongst the flowers with my spring water, cut-glass tumbler and *half a bottle of brandy*, and I am convinced that my despondent and despairing thoughts will evaporate with the morning dew.

I can't wait to try it.

8. Flowers and trees

There is a cosy little village nestling at the foot of the Quantock Hills in Somerset where there is a cottage whose front wall is covered with *Cotoneaster horizontalis*. (Perhaps I should have said there *was* a cosy little village. We haven't been that way for about sixteen years.) This cottage served Afternoon Teas, and as we used to get very hot, hungry and thirsty walking on the Quantocks we were often glad to call in there. We have happy memories of sitting in a small front room, dim and cool, with the quietness of a summer's afternoon broken only by the slow tick of a grandfather clock in the corner of the room, and the constant buzz of bees on that cotoneaster. We drank our tea, and munched buttered scones and jam, whilst sitting beside the open window listening to those bees. 'One day,' we promised ourselves, '*we* shall have a cottage with cotoneaster growing up to the window, so that we can enjoy afternoon tea to the hum of bees.'

On the face of it there didn't seem to be much chance of this dream being realized at Hafod. The stone walls of the cottage and all the outbuildings sat squarely upon the earth, and only grass and nettles grew alongside them. Nowhere were any of the outlines softened by plants that climbed or sprawled. This was, after all, an exposed, wind-torn moorland in North Wales. You couldn't bring Somerset cosiness here. . . . Or could you?

Alan built two small rockeries against the front wall either side of the kitchen window. Between these rockeries he constructed two steps, so that I could stand between the rockeries and clean the kitchen window. He filled the rockeries with some of the best earth he could find, and planted out seedlings of stonecrop, saxifrage and pansies along the stones. He also planted, against the wall, our *Cotoneaster horizontalis* cuttings. The pansies loved it here. They have been growing prettily and

seeding themselves all over the place ever since. The saxifrage
and stonecrop settled in quickly too. Alan built more rockeries.
He built them on either side of the lawn . . . (The 'lawn' is a
square patch of level ground in front of the cottage. As it is the
only bit of level ground we own, we find it a handy place to
repair bikes, sort out the pea netting, clean carpets, etc. We
therefore keep the grass, docks, buttercups, daisies, clovers and
various fungi cut short—by means of a lawn-mower.) . . . and
he also built one at the spring and two by the front door. The
various stonecrops and saxifrages have been divided and spread
around, and they have now taken over. Wherever there are two
or three stones piled together at Hafod, there will be sprawling
rounded cushions of pink, white and yellow, with a few pansies
peeping out here and there, showing cheerful faces of mauve
and black velvet.

But what about the *Cotoneaster horizontalis*?

During the first three years the cuttings sent up a few, thin,
unhappy looking branchlets of not more than five or six inches
in length. The plants flapped about against the wall in the
wind, and didn't seem to grow in height at all. In the meantime
Alan was also planting ivy around the place. The ivy planted
in the rockery by the front door, and in the rockery with the
cotoneaster, made a gallant attempt to cling to the wall. Time
after time its creeping tendrils were torn off by the wind, but
gradually little bits at the base of each plant managed to get a
grip. After a night of storm there were always a lot of plants in
the garden that needed attention, and pruning off the flapping
bits of ivy was a regular job. Gradually the ivy gained strength
and began to creep up the cottage wall. Not only did this give
the cotoneaster encouragement, it also gave it something to
hang on to. Alan wove a few branches in amongst the ivy
tendrils, and the two plants started to grow up the wall together.

If you sit in our kitchen now on a summer's day you can
hear, through the window, a gentle, murmuring buzz. It is the
sound of bees all over the cotoneaster. Come and have a good
look at it. See how strongly it fans across the cottage, bunching
thickly beneath the window-sill, and reaching high up the

walls on either side. What's more, it gives us a bonus. Not only do the bees love it, but also the mistle thrushes. They come each autumn and feed upon the tiny red berries that pepper the branches. We can lean upon our kitchen window-sill and look down upon them as they stand on the rockery and eat the berries. The mistle thrushes have handsome, plump, speckled breasts, but from this angle we see mainly their smooth milk-chocolate backs and the tops of their heads. They don't know that we are watching them, and we chuckle at this happy deception. We back away from the window cautiously so that we don't disturb their meal.

In the meantime, there are other creeping plants taking a hold of the Hafod walls. We planted honeysuckle down by the front gate, in all the hedges, and anywhere else that we thought honeysuckle might be happy. We also planted it beside a small, loosely constructed stone wall that protrudes from the end of the outhouse, and which faces the front door of the cottage. The honeysuckle liked it there, and gradually began to creep up the wall. 'I *must* finish that wall,' Alan said, 'before the honeysuckle covers it.' But there were other things to do; the seasons came and went; and honeysuckle waits for no man. We realized the other day that the small stone wall is no longer to be seen. It is completely covered by a great tangled mound of honeysuckle and roses and ivy. What's more, somewhere inside there—probably against the wall—a wren has built her nest. The honeysuckle is now advancing from the wall and is climbing up the sides of the outhouse itself. 'I *must* repair that guttering,' said Alan, 'before the honeysuckle reaches it.'

The ivy is also taking over. It is climbing strongly up the wall of the shippen and has almost reached the roof in one corner; and it is positively leaping up the stable wall. The stable has a granary which is reached by a sturdy flight of stone and slate steps. On warm summer mornings we like to sit up there with our elevenses. With the sun full upon us and the slates warm beneath us we can sit and gaze down upon things growing in the garden. We noticed the other day that the ivy has now leaped past the steps and is making for the roof. It was also sending out great, strong, green tendrils across the large slate slab at the top of the steps where we were sitting. We had the strong impression that if we hung about too long with our elevenses we should be caught up in those reaching tendrils.

We planted hedges alongside paths, around the vegetable garden and across gaps between buildings to stop the wind tearing through. We have hedges of beech, of Japanese honeysuckle and of privet. We also have mixed hedges of rose, oak, hornbeam, sycamore, hazel and elder. All of them had a struggle to survive, and for many years we had to trim off dead and broken bits, replant, tie up, and generally encourage. Now they are growing strongly. They are Hafod hedges, and can stand up to anything. We keep them well trimmed; sturdy and thick. They reward us by baffling the wind which comes shaking its fist in the tops of the trees, and goes gnashing its teeth up the hillside. It can no longer push us sideways off the paths. The hedges and trees protect us.

The trees which provide most of our shelter are Sitka spruce. The year after we moved in we bought a hundred of them, about 18 inches high, and we planted them in blocks, mainly to the north-west of the cottage. They stand between the cottage and the stable and the spring; also at the far side of the spring, and around the perimeter of the garden fence. For many years they were sad little things, lashing about in the grass, sometimes being torn out by their roots and hurled up the hillside. But gradually they took a hold of the moorland soil and began to grow. We started to fill in with other trees: Scots pine, Japanese larch, Lawson's cypress and various firs. All had a struggle to survive, and some in fact died. But as the years went by and a little shelter was gained, so the trees dug down with their roots and held fast.

The original shaping of the garden, the laying down of paths and the planting of hedges and a shelter belt was all in accordance with a plan. Conceived in Alan's mind, and systematically carried out, the plan gradually fell into place, but he worked with the lie of the land and the feel of the wind when deciding which direction a path should turn or a hedge should curve.

The trees, flowers and shrubs that have come along since have been largely unplanned. They just happened.

Someone gave us some daffodils. We planted them alongside the spring path. We were given some more daffodils—scented ones—and we planted these near the others. More daffodils have come along, and we have planted, split up, replanted and now we have hundreds and hundreds of daffodils along the paths, down by the pond, in and around the trees. We sowed some tree lupins. They now line a bank at the back of the house; a scented row of mauve, yellow and white heads. We have acquired some sweet-williams, phlox and London pride. We bought roses; a moss rose was planted near the back door and the rose Masquerade invited to trail along the vegetable garden fence. We bought crocuses and carnations. But who gave us the double snowdrops? Where did the marguerites come from? Those oriental poppies by the shippen? Did they come from Aunt Daisy, or was it mother? Who gave us the red-hot poker and the rose of Sharon?

Then there have been the plants we rescued. There was that solitary oxlip we snatched almost from the jaws of the bull-dozer in a road-widening scheme. A white melilot was saved at the same time, and a small clump of primroses. But we grieve for the magnificent rare borage. A proud giant with brilliant blue flowers, its stems clothed in handsome black hairs. It was gone when we went back the next day. Smashed flat and churned into the mud. The dyer's green weed that now grows happily upon our bank came from Gloucestershire. It was being destroyed to make way for a car park. The round-leaved mint and the pot marigolds grew in happy profusion upon a site in Somerset destined to be a trading estate. Once again we beat the bulldozers to it. But where did all the others come from? The vetches, the hellebore, vervain, campion and various toad-flax? They weren't here when we came. The years roll by and we forget. But does it really matter? They are Hafod flowers now—growing happily, loved and protected; delighting us by reappearing year after year; sometimes surprising us by seeding themselves and popping up in unlikely corners.

The harebells, yarrow and foxgloves were here already. They grow freely around the place, particularly the foxgloves and yarrow. They like to line the grassy bank alongside the front path and the banks around the vegetable garden. We put up with foxgloves appearing saucily amongst the potatoes. Foxgloves seem to like to be near us as we come and go. There's one growing right now in a crack at the side of the front door threshold. It is a magnificent specimen; a glowing purple spike about three feet high, and it nudges my elbow each time I go out. A foxglove will frequently appear at the entrance to the chicken house, and there is always one at the spring, leaning over to get in the way of my bucket.

We have rescued shrubs and trees as well as flowers. Wherever we have seen machines of 'progress' at work we have endeavoured to remove things from their path. The buddleias were saved in this way. They are covered with blossom each summer, delighting us and the butterflies. Saplings of alder, ash, sycamore, beech, hazel, birch and various elms have been carefully brought home to Hafod and planted inside the fence. Within the protection of the Sitka spruces they have grown and flourished. Some have been coppiced to form a thicket for the birds. Others are being allowed to grow into specimens. Beyond the spring we now have a little wood. Bluebells and primroses grow amongst the trees, and there is a constant rustling of leaves overhead.

To care for the trees means a lot of work. Alan is constantly trimming, pruning, training branches to grow in more convenient positions, and removing undergrowth. The Sitka spruces—growing about six feet apart—are now roof high. Their branches intertwine, and along the spring path they have been trimmed back to form a thick, high hedge, the topmost branches soaring out to provide an overhead shelter. These stands of spruce are now dense and dark, with a soft carpet of needles underfoot. Alan crawls amongst them on hands and knees, pruning off dead bits and cutting back branches that foul each other too much. He comes back into the house smelling of wet woodlands, and with spruce needles in his hair.

Some of our trees are of special significance to us. These are the Scots and Austrian pines, junipers and cedars that Mr. Carr gave us. Mr. Carr was a gentle man. He owned a tree nursery at Gwernymynydd, near Mold. He was an honourable and successful business-man, and he loved trees.

We came to know him when we decided to grow Christmas trees. We had heard that Christmas tree growing was a profitable sideline of valley smallholders and as the making of money has been a perpetual problem with us we decided to enclose a 2-acre plateau at the top of the field and turn it into a Christmas tree plantation. (No one up here on the moors has ever grown Norway spruce, and our proposals brought a lot more head-shaking disapproval from Dilwen.) In the first year of the Hafod Christmas tree enterprise we ordered 2,000 four-year-old Norway spruce from a nurseryman who had been recommended to us by someone we knew in the Forestry Commission. When Alan arrived to collect the trees he found them already waiting for him, tied up in bundles. When he untied the bundles at home he found that the small trees were in very poor shape. Some were without roots, some had branches missing down one side, all were very 'leggy', over half were less than the size ordered, and they were about 160 short in number. Fortunately we hadn't paid for them. We made an appropriate adjustment to the invoice and paid what we considered the trees were worth. The nurseryman didn't argue.

The following year we consulted the telephone directory yellow pages, having decided to buy our next lot of Norway spruce from the tree nursery that happened to be nearest to us. In this way we chanced to select Mr. Carr. It was a happy choice.

Mr. Carr supplied us with 2,000 four-year-old Norway spruce trees each year for three years. He always delivered them and, as Mrs. Carr usually accompanied him, these visits became social occasions. He wanted to know, each time, how the trees were faring. If we reported any losses to him, he brought along replacements. His trees were neat, sturdy and well shaped, and he always threw in a hundred or so extra, 'just in case'. From time to time, when he was passing, he brought us other trees as a gift. 'Thought you might like to grow one of these,' he would say, lifting from the back of his car a specimen of Western hemlock or perhaps an Irish juniper. One year he gave us two kinds of heather for the rockery. All the plants that Mr. Carr gave us are growing strongly at Hafod, but we now care for them with sadness. On the last occasion they visited us, Mrs. Carr mentioned that her husband was waiting to go into hospital for an operation, but that it was being delayed because of the hospital ancillary workers' strike. A couple of months later she wrote to tell us that Mr. Carr was dead.

The Norway Spruce were planted three feet apart in comparatively straight rows across the plateau. Alan did the job on his own, with no tool other than a spade, and no way of measurement other than by eye. This partly accounts for the fact that the rows were only *comparatively* straight. You must also take into account that (a) it goes against Alan's nature to plant anything in straight lines, (b) quite often it was very misty and he was unable to see further than three or four yards and (c) the very action of planting the trees—dig hole, drop in tree, stamp ground, dig hole, drop in tree, stamp ground, and so on —carried out several hundred times per session affected his balance and his eyesight. . . .

The trees were planted in April and, after that, they were forgotten about for a few months, except that the plantation would be visited after strong winds to replant any trees that had blown out of the ground, firm down those that were about to be blown out of the ground, and trim off any dead or broken branches. In the meantime the grass was growing up around them.

The accepted way of keeping grass away from young, growing trees is either to cut the grass or spray it with a herbicide. Well, to begin with, we don't accept that it is *necessary* to keep grass away from young, growing trees. We have read that if grass is allowed to cover their branches it will kill them. We have proved that this is nonsense. In fact, in our situation the grass helps to protect the young trees. Once the grass in the plantation has grown taller than the trees we know that they will stay in the ground no matter how strongly the wind blows. The important thing is not to let the grass die back on to the trees in the winter, otherwise they would be smothered. So the job of disentangling the Christmas trees from the grass became a regular end-of-summer routine for us.

When the trees were small the difficulty was *finding* them amongst the grass. We would stand facing up the field, chest-high in grass, knapweed and ragwort. 'I know I started *some-where* around here,' Alan would say, thrashing about in the grass. As soon as we found the first tree of a row we were all right. We would soon be able to find the one 3 feet to one side of it. Having then uncovered trees at the start of two rows, we were ready to begin. Taking a row each we would work systematically up the field, disentangling the grass from the branches of each tree, flattening the grass all around it, putting weight on the grass—either by kneeling or walking on it—to make sure it stayed down; then shuffling forward to find the next tree. We each had our own method of working. Alan—once he was down upon his knees—stayed down. He would work down the entire length of the plantation on hands and knees. Sometimes I would stand up and be unable to see him. He worked much faster than I did, and would be much further down the field. Then I would spot him, almost hidden by the grass on either side, burrowing away like a mole, leaving a long line of cleared trees standing up jauntily behind him. I was inclined to bob up and down when working. Having flattened the grass with my hands I would stand up and walk around the tree to make sure the grass stayed flat.

As the trees grew and stood way above the tallest grasses, so the difficulties of the job changed. It was no longer a case of not being able to find them, it was a case of getting in close to the tree to clear away the grass from the lower branches, yet avoiding, somehow, getting a spiky branch straight in the eye. So we each wore a pair of wartime anti-gas goggles. But we also found that hands and wrists became very scratched and sore through constant brushing against the branches. So we wore old socks on our hands, pulling the sock legs well up our arms. (Setting off up the field one day, all geared-up for a session in the plantation, we came across Dic climbing over our fence, taking a short-cut to the village. He was unable to speak. Half over the fence, head bowed, hand over face, he was doubled up, shaking uncontrollably with stifled laughter.)

Sometimes, on a warm September day, the plantation is a blissful place to be. When my horizon is reduced to just a few feet and I am cut off from the outside world by a rustling wall of grass and flowers, the little things immediately in front of my nose take my undivided attention, and I see the world as through the eyes of a small creature who scuttles through long grasses. I marvel at tiny toadstools in shades of brown, blue, orange, yellow and white—many like clubs, some like corals and others like fairy coolie hats—all growing under the trees where the grass is dying out; also little feathery mosses with delicate flower stalks upon them. A giant ragwort, gay with tortoise-shell butterflies, looms over me, and a large, fat spider with a striped white body comes out to inspect his web stretched between a harebell plant and the spruce tree—about an inch from my ear.

Once when I was working along my row I discovered a little Norway spruce tree so perfect in shape, so green and so proud that I had to sit back and admire it for a few moments. Then I noticed that there was a nest in the branches. There were four, small, mottled eggs in the nest and I guessed it to be that of a meadow pipit. Had the nest been abandoned? Surely it was much too late in the year for a meadow pipit to be sitting? I wasn't sure, so I hastily replaced some of the tangled grasses over the branches of the tree, and passed on down the row.

When the field is finished and all the grass is flattened neatly we know that the trees stand a good chance of surviving the winter. Snow and ice will lie over the flattened foliage and the trees will be held firmly in the ground.

Norway spruce trees grown in the valley will probably be ready for sale as Christmas trees within three or four years of planting. Up here on the moor they grow much slower, and for year after year we looked after our trees without giving any thought to the selling of them. When six years had passed and some of them were standing nearly three feet high, we decided we should get a 'middleman' to come and look at them and maybe make us an offer. I then realized, somewhat uncomfortably, that the whole prospect of selling our trees was filling me with gloom. All those fine young trees, growing so happily upon that wide, frosty plateau, what was their future to be? I could imagine each tree, stuck in a bucket next to the television set in someone's centrally heated lounge. Festooned with lights and packages, it would be the centre of attention for about three weeks, and then out it would go—alongside the dustbin, to await its final journey in the garbage cart. Never mind little tree! Abandon your meadow pipit's nest; shake off your spider; we are going to give you a nice plastic fairy!

The man came. He went up to the plantation with Alan. The man went away, and Alan came back poker-faced. 'Well, what did he say?' 'He kicked them around a bit, said they were too small, and offered me fivepence each for them. I told him we wouldn't sell.' My gloom lifted. Everything was going to be all right. For at least another year our trees would be up there on the hill, along with the wind, the grass and the skylarks.

We now don't know how many trees we have growing at Hafod. But there are so many that it is possible for us to lose each other amongst them. I may go to the spring, and get side-tracked into wandering downstream to look at the pond; or I may go up to the wych-elm plot to hang out my washing and stay there sitting in the sun looking at the hills. A trip down to the front gate to collect the post will mean dallying along the lower path by the hawthorn hedge in order to sniff the sweet rockets. 'Oh *there* you are,' Alan will say, 'I've been looking everywhere for you.'

A walk in the woodland brings its own special delights. There are the shifting patterns of light and shade; there are secret flitting movements of birds, and there is a hushed tranquillity of trees moving gently in a light wind. There are also the scents—the fresh smell of damp earth and larch trees, the more elusive fragrance of gorse on the hill behind us, and the faint sweetness of the rose hedging. But the woodland has also a certain 'feeling' beyond that to which our senses respond. It now has a spirit of its own, and there is a threshold of understanding which, in moments of quiet, we can sometimes cross.

Why do so many people recognize only mature trees? Clumsy visitors sometimes walk upon our saplings of ash and sycamore without even noticing. And I shudder to think just how many healthy little trees up and down the country have been destroyed by well-meaning 'conservationists'. We know of two schools that, between them, managed to get rid of scores of trees as their contribution to 'Conservation Year'. In the first school the headteacher decided that the senior boys should 'tidy up' a length of river bank. What had previously been a tangle of hawthorn, elder and bramble bushes (discreetly covering the old prams, abandoned cars and general junk that lay beneath) became a muddy desert under the enthusiastic hatchets of the boys. Admittedly the boys also disposed of the old prams, cars and general junk, but I wonder what happened to all the nesting birds and other creatures that must have been there? Fortunately, the boys didn't make a very good job of it. The last time we went that way the river bank was beginning to re-clothe itself—which is just as well—because the rusty spin-dryers, old mattresses, broken chairs and abandoned cookers are putting in an appearance again.

The primary school made a much more thorough job of destruction. The children were invited to collect money to buy a tree. The local council gave permission for the school to plant their tree in an overgrown area of the nearby park. In preparing the ground to receive their tree, the children pulled up many sapling sycamores, birch, ash and rowan trees, and the school caretaker made a bonfire of them on the patch of ground.

Later on the children planted *their* tree—a flowering cherry.

Perhaps it is not fair of me to quote these two instances without qualification. Undoubtedly there are many groups of young people all over the country who are working hard to protect what is left of our flora and fauna . . . which is just as well. If there *is* any hope for the future, it can only lie with the young. But I think it is a great pity when children's enthusiasm for 'nature' is directed to improvements, such as planting new trees, without being taught to *see what is already there* and making informed decisions on which plants and animals should be cherished, and which, if any, should be sacrificed in the interests of the community (and I mean them—the plants and animals —as well as us).

However, it is certainly heartening that so many people these days are concerned at the disappearance of so much that is beautiful and interesting in the British countryside, and we are happy when we hear of councils being bullied by local people into preserving banks of rare flowers, or trees that are much-loved landmarks. Small groups of dedicated people can and do stop acts of vandalism by local government officials.

I suppose that what annoys us most is the commonly made mistake of confusing tidying-up with conservation. In an official publication issued recently by the planning department of a large city, there was a pair of 'before' and 'after' photographs proudly labelled 'Successful conservation scheme on derelict site'. The first photograph showed a large patch of land, with houses on three sides. This land appeared to be covered with rubbish, scrubby bushes, grass and nettles, and I could see one or two large plants of evening primrose and chicory in the foreground. The whole area was undoubtedly an irritation to local people, a veritable eyesore where children got up to mischief, adolescents 'carried on' in the bushes and adults dumped their junk. The second picture illustrated the area after the council bulldozers had been at work. The land had been levelled, sown with grass seed and planted with trees (flowering cherries I'll bet!). There were several seats scattered around, and the whole area had now become a patch of land that was easy on the eye and a place where old people could sit in the sun and keep an eye upon the goings-on of the young. A thoroughly worthwhile and commendable clearing-up operation had been carried out. The only mistake was in labelling it 'conservation' because, in order to improve his own habitat man had, in the process, destroyed the habitats of countless plants, and probably of a few animals too.

You will perhaps now understand why we felt somewhat unenthusiastic at 'plant a tree' year. When Muriel came up our garden path with her collecting box we tried to explain all this to her. But, as usual, she wasn't listening. 'I thought you were supposed to *like* trees,' she said.

9. Mostly about manure

Dic was standing at the front gate. He gave a small cough to attract my attention, and I looked up. We normally keep the front gate padlocked to discourage casual callers; that is, the kind of callers who, claiming some vague acquaintance with us from our previous town life, come cadging afternoon tea. 'We are on holiday up here . . . thought we'd look you up. Ho ho, ho ho!' The local people know that we keep the gate locked, and they also know that it is not them we are trying to keep out. So they either sit in their car and honk their horn (like Muriel), or they just climb over the gate (like Dic and Dilwen). But climbing over someone's front gate just isn't done if that someone is standing in the garden within sight. This is why Dic was leaning on the gate, grinning and coughing. 'Would Mr. West like some manure?' he asked.

What Dic really meant was that their bullocks, having been shut up in an outbuilding for all the winter, and part of the spring, had now been let out, and he wanted us to come and help with the almighty task of removing a knee-high layer of manure from the outbuilding and stacking it in the yard. Reward for this work would be half a van-load of manure for the garden at Hafod, and this was always welcome.

The winters in this Welsh upland are always long, and sometimes severe. So the cattle are usually brought in from the moorland at the onset of cold weather and penned near the house. When conditions are very bad they are housed—sometimes for weeks on end—in cowsheds. When winter is over and the fields are beginning to stir and awaken with a light covering of new green growth, the cattle are released from their winter quarters. They come galloping across the fields, jumping, bucking and leaping with joy. We have seen our neighbours' cattle charging about like children released from school. However, they soon settle down to the serious business of feeding and, apart from the occasional mild punch-up with each other, these sturdy little beasts with their glossy black coats will spend the summer roaming freely and calmly amongst the gorse and bracken on the boulder-strewn hillsides.

The manure from the cowsheds is normally transferred straight away to the fields. The land up here needs this manure, and so we are particularly grateful when our neighbours give us a load because we know that they really should be putting it on their own land. However, Dic and Dilwen don't seem to be too bothered about transferring muck to the fields. Most of it remains in a huge pile just outside the back door, so we never feel guilty about having as much of it as we can.

'Yes please,' I replied, 'Shall we come along this afternoon?'

I particularly remember that visit. Not only was it the day the cattle were released, it was also the day the pig was imprisoned—and this was a performance that took up most of the afternoon, and all of the energies of Dic, Dilwen and sister Gwen, whilst Alan and I tackled the manure.

We realized that something was going on as soon as we arrived. There was no one in the yard, and the back door was open. But there were distant sounds of some sort of hullabaloo on the hillside behind the house. The cowshed door was open, and the manure was there waiting for us—a couple of feet thick, and trampled down hard. The dozen bullocks that had been released from this small shed were standing around the yard, bleary-eyed, bewildered and with dung plastered about their flanks. No joyful leaping around here. We gained the impression that it had been so long since these beasts had seen open country that they were a bit nervous of it. We wondered why they were still penned in the yard. We also wondered about the hullabaloo that was gradually coming closer. We took our forks from the van and started digging out manure from the doorway of the shed. (Dic and Dilwen don't seem to possess many hand tools, and I knew that the only implements they had for this sort of work were one very large shovel with a long handle, and a small spade with a jaggedly broken handle.

As I guessed that handling the small jagged-handled spade would be *her* work, I made sure that our garden forks were on board the van before we drove over.) We had hardly got started on this work when there rushed into the yard a very large and pregnant pig, closely followed by Dic wielding a long stick, and Gwen carrying a large black and steaming kettle. The pig bowled straight through the group of bullocks (one of which stepped neatly out of the way into the kitchen) and blundered past us into the cowshed. The pig was not supposed to go into the cowshed, but no amount of beating by Dic would persuade her to come out. Gwen, clambering awkwardly over the manure, went to his assistance with her kettle of hot water. This proved to be much more effective because there was a sudden loud squeal, and with a flurry of whizzing manure, the pig came hurtling out of the doorway again, and made straight for the gate. She reached it just before Dilwen (who was coming in with the two dogs) managed to close it; there was a mêlée of pig, dogs and Dilwen at the gate, and then suddenly they were all off again up the hillside.

Alan and I carried on digging out manure.

We were told the full story later in the day when we were all having tea. The pig, we gathered, was about to have her litter. She wasn't going to be allowed to give birth in the fields, neither was she going to be allowed the full use of an out-building, because if she could move freely she might trample or roll upon her piglets as they were born. She had, therefore, to be confined, lying on her side, in a wooden crate. She would stay that way until the pigs were born, and until they were big enough to be able to get out of her way as she lumbered about. The piglets, nipping in and out of the bars of the crate, would have unhindered access to Mum, who just lay there—a large, immobile milk bar, taking all her food and relieving herself in that prone position for maybe several weeks. This particular mother pig had been through all this before. She knew what was coming to her. Quite naturally, she was anxious to take to the hills.

'She's a very good pig, that one,' said Gwen, carefully wiping away a small piece of manure that had fallen from her hair on to the breadboard, 'She gave us a litter of thirteen last year, so she's worth looking after. Now. Who's for some more bread and jam?'

Most of the manure we are given goes to the potato crop. If we can spare any, then the fruit bushes will get some. We notice that, when referring to manure, our books insist that it must be 'well rotted'. We don't really understand this. If manure is left to lie around in order to rot, surely some of the goodness (if that's the right word) will be washed or dried out of it? Any manure we are able to get hold of goes straight from the cowshed on to the garden and, so far as we are able to see, the results are wholly beneficial. But we cannot rely upon getting manure, and many years we are without it. So we make compost.

A lot has been written about making compost. Most gardening books have something to say on the subject. But, like most other aspects of gardening, we found that the advice didn't apply to us at Hafod. To begin with, we find that compost takes much longer to rot down. A heap which in the lowlands would rot down into usable material in, say, a year would take three years up here. This means that we find it necessary to have three compost heaps in the garden at the same time: the one we are currently building, the one we topped up to leave standing last year, and the one we completed building the year before that—and which will be ready for use next year. When, in the spring, we open up a compost heap for use, the whole lot will be disposed of, mainly to the peas, beans and potatoes. And the site of the compost heap will be one of the richest parts of the garden.

Being in such urgent need of compost all the time, we make sure that nothing compostable is wasted. All vegetable peelings, grass cuttings, weeds and fallen leaves are added to the pile, along with cut-up pieces of old clothes (so long as they are either cotton or wool), flock from any abandoned mattresses, feathers from cushions, bits of leather and, of course, the contents of The Bucket. We try to arrange that the heap is built in layers, with an occasional dressing of soot or lime. When, after three years, it is opened it will be full of worms and none of the original contents will be recognizable, except eggshells.

Our mumbo-jumbo gardening book had quite a lot to say about the making of compost. The whole performance was surrounded with an aura of mystique, without which, we gathered, the compost was not likely to be of much use. One should endeavour to have the compost heap situated underneath an elder tree because there were special secretions from the roots (I would have thought it far more likely that the elder tree was lapping up the special secretions from the compost heap), and one should sprinkle it with fresh herbs. Well, certainly; any trimmings from our herb bushes go on to the compost heap, but I'm not convinced they do any more for the heap than our weeds, vegetable peelings or pea pods. But it was the curious things you had to do with your comfrey leaves that puzzled us. One should, apparently, chop them up, put them in a barrel and cover them with water, then just leave the barrel standing for a few months, sometimes adding more comfrey, and occasionally giving it a good stir. The resultant fluid was a marvellous liquid manure for your crops. Perhaps it is. But what's wrong with putting your comfrey leaves on the compost heat? We do—several times a year—because we find that the comfrey plants all love a good chop every now and then, and they will send up a whole jungle of massive new leaves as a reward.

We once visited an exhibition where an experimental 'organic garden' had been laid out. We were shown around by a rather sad, long-haired, limp-wristed youth who pointed out to us the crops that had been fed with watery comfrey, those that had been fed with artificial fertilizers, and those that had received nothing. He needed to point them out because, so far as we could see, they all looked the same—shrunken, half-starved and far from happy. The crops looked very similar to some of the vegetables in our early days at Hafod, before we had improved the soil and gained some shelter. This 'organic garden' was several hundred feet lower than us in altitude and was not in need of shelter, but the soil was the same, poor, thin, stony rubbish that we had started with. Before coming to any conclusions about their 'organic' experiment, these earnest young people should take a walk along the road and look at the gardens of their neighbours in the council houses. The healthy great potato haulms, squat fat turnips and the runner bean sticks completely buried beneath tangled vines festooned with long bunches of beans, seem to indicate that, whatever the problems of the local soil, the council house tenants have overcome them.

I must confess to being rude about watery comfrey without having actually tried it—which is, perhaps, unfair. But, having experimented (briefly) with chemical fertilizers I feel that I can be as rude as I like about them. One year we gave half of the vegetables in our garden two doses of a well-known general fertilizer in the correct quantities, according to the instructions on the bag. (Of each separate crop, half of the vegetables had fertilizer and half didn't.) They were all growing in the same patch of ground and all were equally exposed to sun, rain and wind. By the end of the year we had proved to our satisfaction that putting chemical fertilizers upon our garden was a sheer waste of money. There was no difference whatsoever between the vegetables that were given fertilizer and those that weren't —not in speed of growth, nor size of crop. We are now convinced that hard work, plenty of compost and occasional manure are the first three requirements of a vegetable garden, but that in the end it all depends upon the weather anyway.

In spite of being extremely compost-conscious and wasting absolutely nothing that would help to increase the size of our heaps, we can never make enough of it. This sometimes results in the soil taking on a patchy appearance, which is particularly noticeable after a couple of years of not giving it any manure. The only sure way of getting manure is to keep animals. This we have been unable to do because of our somewhat nomadic lifestyle, and we are very much aware of the resultant one-sidedness of our life at Hafod. We know there is something missing. There should be a few hens scratching about under the trees; perhaps a duck or two paddling about in the pond and a goat browsing up there amongst the gorse on the hillside. But we are not financially secure here. We have found no reliable way of making a living, and we are never quite sure how long we can stay here at one stretch before we have to go away for a few weeks, or even months. The longest unbroken stretch of time that we have lived here without having to go away is four and a half years. In that time we could have kept several generations of hens and reared a couple of goats. But what then? Give them away? Send them to be slaughtered? No. Any animal of ours *must* be assured of a safe and happy life. Until we can offer it security, there will be no animal of ours at Hafod.

At one time we considered keeping animals for purely mercenary reasons. A pig, for example. We have a stone-built sty all ready for it. According to Dic and Dilwen a lot of money can be made from a pig. And then we would have plenty of manure too. So we bought a book on pig-keeping—and changed our minds. Keeping a pig was not a happy, straightforward affair of throwing it scraps and tickling its back and chatting it up over the pigsty gate. You had to do things like castrating the piglets and cutting their teeth, and giving them all sorts of injections against disease. Anyway, who were we fooling? We could never send all those delightful creatures to the slaughterer!

For similar reasons of cowardice we also decided against keeping a cow. We were then left with the uncomfortable task of living with ourselves having discovered that, though not wanting to get involved in the nastiness and treachery of farming animals, we were still prepared to eat meat. We still haven't come to terms with this. In the meantime we carry on eating meat (albeit only occasionally—we can't afford it very often) and feeling uncomfortable.

No such doubts troubled me as a child. I was the youngest in a family of six; it was wartime and we had a large garden. We kept hens; we always had a few cockerels fattening up; sometimes we kept a couple of ducks, and we always had rabbits. Helping to look after the animals was my particular delight.

Cleaning out the rabbits was no chore for me. We kept Flemish Giants and Chinchillas, and I loved handling them. I would talk to them, kiss and cuddle them. And the next day I tucked into rabbit stew without a care in the world. Dad would kill a rabbit when one was needed for the pot, and he nailed its skin on the back of the shed door. When a dozen or so skins had accumulated, they would be sent away for dressing. Back they would come, soft and smelling sweetly. The winter evenings were spent making fur-backed gloves. Dad did the cutting out of the leather and fur, Mum assembled all the bits and hand-sewed the leather and fur, and the rest of us helped with sewing up the linings. But it was Mum's fingers that did most of the real work. The gloves she made were handsome to look at, warm and comfortable to wear and beautiful to feel— and they sold faster than she could make them.

Feeding the animals each evening was a job that I found entirely satisfying. We had two large old saucepans in which we boiled up all vegetable peelings and leftovers. This lot was transferred to a large galvanized bucket, and a quantity of fawn-coloured powder called 'balancer meal' was added. The contents of the bucket were then chopped up and transferred to a couple of old meat tins (for the fowl run) with some of it being retained to roll up into balls (about tennis ball size), one of which was given to each rabbit. Having done this, I would just wander around and watch them all eating. All those gobbling and gulping beaks, and all those nuzzly, munching jaws made me smile to myself with pleasure. I was enjoying all the delights of owning animals, and experiencing none of the doubts. (I wasn't a particularly bright child and I didn't have an enquiring mind. When, as a result of my obvious energy and enthusiasm, I was encouraged to breed guinea-pigs 'to sell to the university' never once did it occur to me to question what the university wanted them for. I knew that the university was a very posh and important place and I assumed that my guinea-pigs were fulfilling some posh and important purpose.)

Breeding rabbits for commercial purposes was another scheme we considered at Hafod. The shippen could be adapted for this quite easily with the walls lined with cages and a large area of the floor fenced off as a 'free-range' area. We could even arrange a free-range area on the lawn, with access gained from the back of the shippen. There is a slowly growing market for rabbit meat and we even found a middleman prepared to buy all our output in the form of live rabbits, thus pandering to our cowardice and relieving us of all of the nastiness of the business. We have not taken this idea any further because the scheme wouldn't in itself support us, and we are still searching for that other 'secure' source of income. But we shall bear it in mind for the future.

Keeping rabbits would be an admirable way for the sub-urban gardener to ensure a non-stop supply of manure for his garden. According to information in a booklet on the subject, rabbit manure contains more nitrogen, phosphoric acid and potash than farmyard manure. Poultry manure, I understand, is even more nutritious. So if a man has enough room to house a couple of rabbits and half a dozen hens, his soil-improving problems are over.

I would like to see a return of this back-garden smallholding in towns—and a return of the mateyness between men who swapped seed potatoes, beans and peas and lent each other prize bucks or cocks to ensure the continuance of a healthy line of rabbits and poultry. People's gardens were so much more interesting then; untidy, maybe, with sheds, old boxes, things in sacks and bits of wire netting, but at least these gardens gave the impression that the people there were *living*, not just sitting around waiting for something to happen. And if this sort of backyard husbandry can be combined with a cottage industry such as glove making, or soft-toy making, surely this would give an added dimension to family life?

Perhaps all these excellent ideas sound a little hollow, coming from someone like me who has no children and is sitting up here on the moorland owning several acres of rough grazing out the back, and surrounded by solid stone-built animal houses that are filled with 'useful junk'.

So what are we going to do about it?

We can only hope for better things in the future, and make plans for that time when we can eventually feel settled here.

I have this little day-dream about goats. I can see the stable all nice and cosy with a thick layer of bracken bedding, and two gentle nanny-goats. (The stable is a fine stone building with a cobbled floor and already fitted with hay racks. There are two bays in it and plenty of room for the storing of foodstuffs.) We have known several goats—and gentle, sweet-natured creatures they were too. My goats will be loving and obedient, but in-clined to be naughty, in the way that all goats are. I shall lead them out of the stable and take them through the little wood-land and out on to the hillside. They will probably attempt to snatch at a few trees on the way, but I shall smack their bottoms and pull them onwards. Until we can afford to spend a lot of money on improving fences, my goats will have to be tethered. But it will be a long tether, and anyway, I shall spend a lot of time up there on the hillside with them, and when I am there they won't need a tether. We shall have to grow some extra root crops for the goats, but as there will be plenty of manure, this should be no problem. There are, however, a few faint clouds in my daydream. In order to have milk from my goats, they must occasionally have babies. We could obviously cope with a couple of kids, and even one billy-goat maybe. But what about the others as they came along? Eat them? I know that we couldn't. We shall probably be able to give away or sell the female kids, but not the males. The most sensible answer would be to kill all male kids soon after birth. But I can't quite bring myself to face up to that one. Not just yet.

Then, of course, there will be the poultry. Not many; perhaps just a half a dozen hens and a few Old English Game bantams. We shall have the bantams (say, three hens and a cock) be-cause they are so proud and pretty. The chicken house is not such a good building as the stable, and we are not absolutely sure that we could keep flood water and rats out of it. So we shall make separate little wooden houses for our poultry—these houses being positioned inside the existing chicken house. (Alan has already started work on the bantam house.)

I would also like to have some ducks. Just a pair maybe. I know they will probably trample about on our pond-side flowers, and they will most certainly gobble up a lot of the tadpoles and small frogs. But I still think it would be nice to have some ducks.

And perhaps we'll think again about that rabbit scheme.

I have no illusions about the amount of work all this is going to involve; all the humping about of food, carrying buckets of water, and shovelling of muck. But I remember my childhood feelings of satisfaction; and I would like to enjoy all those feelings again, please.

And just think of all that manure!

But, in the meantime, we carry on making compost, and cadging from Dic and Dilwen.

10. What pests?

We once sprayed a Scots pine tree with a pyrethrum solution. It was an emergency. We had returned after an absence of several weeks to find this tree infested with a small caterpillar resembling that of the gooseberry sawfly. This is our most important Scots pine tree. It stands alone upon a little tump (as all Scots pines should) between the stable and the bottom pond. It is a strong and proud tree now, standing higher than the stable, but it was a sorry sight when it was covered with caterpillars. The lower branches were completely denuded of leaves, and the millions of munching jaws were slowly working their way up the tree. Caterpillars were covering it as far as the eye could see—and well out of our reach. Desperate measures were called for. We bought some pyrethrum straight away; mixed a solution in a bucket, and got cracking with the stirrup pump. The tree was saved. We used the rest of the pyrethrum (over the course of the next few years) on our gooseberry bushes because they occasionally get attacked by the sawfly. We have never bought any more pyrethrum; it has not been necessary. The caterpillars that visit our gooseberry bushes from time to time can be easily picked off by hand.

This is the only time we have resorted to a pesticide in the garden. We chose pyrethrum because it is a vegetable product, and somehow seemed less nasty than some obscure compound of questionable chemicals. (We realize that the decision was an emotional one.) I do not wish to sound self-righteous over this question of pesticides. Our pests are few and we normally have no trouble controlling them, but I can well imagine the murderous thoughts of a gardener who gets up each morning to find rows of seedlings eaten to the ground by slugs and snails, and the blackfly covering his broad beans. Destruction by any

means available seems a natural response. I am just very relieved that we don't have to face these problems.

(It would be very interesting to make a cost and quantity
comparison between the produce of our garden up here on the
moors, and one of similar size in the lowlands. Our growing
season is shorter and cooler, therefore we are likely to produce
smaller and fewer vegetables and fruit. We have few pests, but
we might suffer damage to crops because of severe weather. On
the other hand, the lowland gardener, who will produce more
and bigger vegetables and fruit, will lose quite a lot through
pests, or have to spend money on pesticides. I wonder which of
us will end the year with the most food—and at what cost?)

I may be prepared to keep an open mind on the subject of
pesticides, but it is completely closed when it comes to herbi-
cides. I can find no justification for them whatsoever. They are
likely to be dangerous, they are certainly unpleasant, the full
effects of their use are probably underestimated and, I suspect,
not properly understood. And they are not even efficient!
Furthermore, I cannot believe that anyone can really prefer to
see brown dead weeds rather than live green weeds. If you
really don't like to see a weed or a bank of lush grass at the
roadside, what is wrong with digging it out or cutting it down?

Alan spent his childhood living on a council housing estate
where the gardens are hedged with privet and all the footpaths
are edged with a grass verge. He remembers that *one man* was
employed to keep the outsides of the hedges trimmed, the grass
verges cut and the weeds removed from between the paving
stones. He cut the hedges with a sickle, he trimmed the grass
with a scythe and he removed the weeds from between the
paving slabs with a long gouge-like implement. He appeared
to be a happy man, Alan remembers, and the estate was always
tidy. Now the job is done by teams of bad-tempered, 'transistor-
ized' young men who descend upon the estate on three or four
occasions during the summer. They do not cut the hedges (this
is now the tenant's responsibility), the grass is roughly cut by
power mowers (which frequently skim off the grass down to the
soil) and they don protective clothing and masks to walk

around the roads broadcasting poison spray and Radio One with equal abandon. The weeds remain as brown lumps in the pathways for people to trip over, and gardeners aren't very happy about weed-killer that floats over the hedge.

I suppose that until some bold council comes up with a new idea (like employing men with hand tools?) that all the other councils will follow—they *do* copy each other, have you noticed? —our local government employees will carry on playing about with these dangerous toys. I only hope they don't come near Hafod.

Returning to the pests at Hafod, they are so few and far between that we accept them as part of our community and are in fact quite interested to observe them. Take snails, for example. For the first five years we were here we didn't see any. Then, one day, I found one sleeping between two stones in the front garden bank. 'Come and see what I've found,' I said, fetching Alan, 'Look! A snail!' We peered with interest. Yes, it seemed to be alive. We checked up on it the next day. Yes, it had moved, but it was still near the same place. We hoped that no thrush would find our snail. We wondered if it would find a mate. We have no idea what it ate; it certainly never went near the vegetable garden. Slugs, too, are a rarity. We sometimes find a few small ones in the soil of the vegetable garden, but we haven't noticed any damage to crops. Our most common slug is that large, handsome black one. On wet evenings they come out from the long grass and take a walk down the spring path. We occasionally see them feeding upon a shrub or a flower, but there are not enough of them to worry us and, once again, they seem to do no damage in the vegetable garden.

Leatherjackets, millipedes, wireworms—we get a few of these, and sometimes we find an earwig or two amongst the lettuces, but the few aphids that visit us are kept in check by the birds. It is pleasant to lean on the garden gate watching the blue tits doing the rounds of the broad beans, acrobatically examining the undersides of all the leaves just to make quite sure there isn't one tiny insect they missed.

We sometimes get a bit of trouble with cabbage root fly, but

if Alan notices it early enough he can usually save the plant by
lifting it carefully without damaging the roots, then washing
off the earth and grubs thoroughly in the spring, and replanting
it somewhere else in the garden. (We have never had more
than two or three plants affected at one time.) Carrot fly took
us longer to deal with. Year after year our carrots were affected
sometimes quite badly. We tried all the herbal concoctions
(watering with boiled-up brews and sprinkling with dried and
fresh herbs) without success. Then one year we tried growing
them in the front garden, well away from the vegetable garden.
They were perfect. We have grown them there ever since, and
they have not been affected by the carrot fly grubs. Have we
by chance found the correct collection of 'sympathetic' com-
panions for our carrots? I don't know. But, for what it's worth,
I will list the surrounding plants. The carrots are always sown
now in a bed alongside the strawberry patch, with parsley,
marjoram, thyme and rosemary growing nearby; also a line of
blackcurrant bushes and some gooseberry bushes.

There were very few black ants and no red ones when we
came to Hafod, but the black ones seem to have increased in
numbers, and red ones have appeared. What fascinating creatures they are to watch. We have one ant 'township' in a
border behind some stones. We once watched them on a day
of great excitement. Ants were rushing about hither and
thither over the stones, with an occasional winged ant putting
in an appearance. If you managed to keep track of one ant you
could see that it was running backwards and forwards or in
circles, and every time it came face to face with a colleague it
would stop and they would put out their front legs and touch
each other. We gained the impression that they were passing
some sort of message. One day, when I was washing some
seakale beet in the kitchen an ant ran out from a leaf on to my
arm. I went outside and dropped it on to one of the stones near
this ant township. Guessing that this particular ant probably
didn't come from that particular community, I waited to see
what would happen. The ant walked about, a little cautiously,
and then suddenly another ant appeared from between the

stones. The two ants faced each other and there was this touching of front legs. Then more ants appeared and surrounded the pair. They all seemed to be examining the newcomer. Then, with my ant in their midst, they all went back between the stones. It was quite obviously a case of 'Take me to your leader'.

Moles and short-tailed voles are sometimes a bit of a nuisance. I hope that the mole is doing all sorts of Good Works underground by eating any slugs or leatherjackets that he comes across, but he is also gobbling up our worms (and we haven't all that many) and he undermines our crops. We have lost young hedging plants that mole has trundled beneath, and he has caused havoc amongst the vegetable seedlings. We have tried to persuade him to go away by many methods, both practical and cranky, but none has worked. We have tried pushing unpleasant things down his runs, like gorse and mole traps, and we have planted them with caper spurge and tree onions. The mole—we had read—doesn't like caper spurge and tree onions. The book was right; the mole doesn't. So he shoved them out of the way and carried on tunnelling. If we persistently stamp down his runs he sometimes gets fed up and moves to another part of the garden but, after a while, he will be back again. On the whole he can be classed as one of our biggest nuisances.

The short-tailed voles generally live in and around the uncultivated parts of the garden, but occasionally they come and lark about in the vegetable garden. They too make underground runs, and they aren't above eating a few leaves, nibbling at an occasional artichoke or potato and snatching the odd pea pod that hangs to the ground. Alan once came across a whole colony of them living in a patch of kale that had become rather overgrown. The voles were running around in and out of their holes, nibbling a few leaves, chittering and arguing with each other and completely ignoring Alan as he stood over them. The voles were probably amazed when they found themselves being picked up and tossed into the long grass outside the vegetable garden. Alan moved five of them in this way. He then tidied up the kale plants, removing all dead and unwanted lower leaves, so that the ground around each plant was fully exposed. This removal of cover would not have appealed to the voles one bit—and they didn't come back.

We seem to have quite a healthy balance of predator and prey amongst our population of wild creatures and, because of this, our pests are controlled without us having to do anything but stand aside and cheer them all on. Our ponds produce an abundance of frogs who live happily in and around the garden, gobbling up flies, slugs, grubs and insects in passing. Unfortunately the frogs are themselves pursued by a rather vicious weasel who lives in the front bank, but as the weasel also chases the mice and voles we can forgive him. We also have a handsome stoat who eats frogs, mice and voles, and kills the occasional mole. Moles, apparently, don't taste very nice because I have never known a stoat eat an entire mole. We usually find their bloody remains deposited on the path. The king of our carnivores is, of course, the polecat who took up winter quarters in our shippen; as he also likes frogs, mice and voles, he obviously wouldn't allow the weasel and stoat families to get too uppity.

We have been able to watch the stoat quite closely all year round. We find that if we stand still when he is pottering about in the garden he will come quite close (within a few feet) and peer at us curiously. We were standing by the vegetable garden gate one afternoon when we became aware of an uproar going on in the elder shrubbery near the back door. Something was obviously chasing something else. Suddenly a large frog came leaping out from the elder bushes. Two frantic leaps and he was sitting trembling upon my sandalled foot. He was closely pursued by stoat, who gave a sort of skidding somersault when he saw us and, chittering with frustrated rage, he raced up and down on either side of us (coming to within eighteen inches of our feet) squealing with anger and greed, yet still held back by fear. The frog—who seemed to know exactly what he was doing —just sat there on my foot. I feel sure that if we had not moved, stoat would have eventually seized the frog from my foot. But as he seemed to be darting in closer Alan shuffled his feet and told him to push off. Stoat disappeared into the elder shrubbery again, but we could hear him in there, hopping up and down with rage and pouring out a non-stop stream of stoat invective at us.

If we didn't have our resident carnivores I am sure we would have more trouble with rabbits and hares. Though happy to watch these delightful creatures frolicking upon the hillside—and what could be more entertaining than a boxing match between two hares?—we weren't quite so eager to see their goings-on in the vegetable garden. The rabbits come more frequently, but they do less damage. We once watched a baby rabbit hopping happily down the main path inside the vegetable garden. He took a few bites from a lettuce leaf, then wandered further along to chew a groundsel down to the ground. He sniffed at the onions, didn't like them, so he ate a raspberry leaf instead. Then he found the kale, and sat there to eat a leaf. But on he went immediately afterwards and started on the chickweed. We decided to chase him out of the garden simply because we thought he might stay there happily munching away until he became too fat to squeeze out through the fencing again.

When a hare decides to come into the vegetable garden, *nothing* can keep him out. Hares have a *thing* about broccoli, and once a hare has discovered that we have some in the garden, then we might as well give up all thoughts of broccoli for dinner. Hares can jump over our 3-foot-high wire netting around the vegetable garden without any bother at all, but we are completely baffled as to how they get through or over the main fence between the Hafod garden and field. This fence is made of 4-inch mesh sheep netting 3 feet 6 inches high, reinforced with 2-inch mesh netting. But the overall height of the fence is increased to about 4 feet 6 inches by a looped tangle of barbed wire on top. We have tried protecting individual broccoli plants with a tangle of wire netting around them, but somehow or other the hare manages to squeeze underneath and still get at the plant. Fortunately for us, hares are comparatively rare visitors, otherwise we should have to give up growing broccoli.

On the whole we are quite happy to share Hafod with the present population of insects and small mammals. They sometimes exasperate us, but we know that during the course of the year their attacks on our crops won't make a lot of difference to the total amount of food we shall eventually harvest. This benevolent attitude of ours does not, however, apply to the biggest nuisance of all . . . the sheep. If a sheep got into the garden and remained unnoticed for any length of time we know that we could lose everything.

The most widespread breed of sheep in Wales is the Welsh Mountain. It is the smallest breed in Britain, yet one of the hardiest, for it thrives upon scrubby and meagre vegetation and withstands harsh climatic conditions. These are facts that no one would dispute. But I feel that I can add to them. Not only is the Welsh Mountain sheep the smallest and hardiest breed, it is also the craftiest. It knows that it can thrive upon scrubby and meagre vegetation, but it doesn't see why it should have to when there is an alternative—like a garden full of luscious green vegetables. And the sheep of Hiraethog, given half a chance (and a hole in the fence), will supplement their diet with Hafod crops at any opportunity.

In our experience, sheep will eat *anything*. They will chew a path of destruction from their point of entry through the fence and across the wych-elm plot, or through the woodland, to the vegetable garden—which is their main objective. They will eat anything *en route*: shrubs, trees, herbs, rhubarb, flowers, and still have enough appetite left to polish off one kale plant after another.

This entirely unselective greed of the sheep is hotly disputed by Dic and Dilwen who both claim vehemently that sheep don't eat trees. For a long time now they have been trying to persuade us to allow their sheep into our Christmas tree plantation 'to keep the grass down'. 'But they will eat the trees,' we protested. 'Oh no they won't,' Dic said, 'Sheep don't eat trees; it's the wool that kills them.' 'They do say,' Dilwen explained, 'that if some wool gets on to a branch and you leave it there for a long time, the tree will die. It is something in the wool they say.' Dilwen was delighted when, a few days after this conversation, he was able to make his point more emphatically. He was giving Alan a lift to Llanrwst in his van, when they passed a small Forestry Commission plantation into which the sheep had obviously broken. Dilwen stamped on the brakes and they got out to have a closer look. There were the remains of a dozen or so small conifers (probably Sitka spruce) that had obviously been eaten almost to the ground. Only the main stalks remained, with just a few stubby, needle-covered knobs to indicate where the young branches had stuck out. 'There you are,' said Dilwen triumphantly pointing to a few wisps of wool adhering to one or two of them, 'What did I tell you!'

Having now lived surrounded by sheep for thirteen years we have come to appreciate some hidden depths in these very-much-taken-for-granted creatures. We have read that the sheep of the particular breed found in the Celtic parts of Britain have several primitive characteristics which suggest that they may be direct descendants of the sheep of pre-Roman Britain. (Not only the sheep have remained unchanged down the centuries; Iron Age and Roman sheep shears were identical in pattern to those still used for handshearing today. . . . We found a pair at Hafod, hanging in the shippen.) Have you ever noticed the way sheep follow each other very carefully along their narrow tracks across the fields and the open hillside? They observe certain crossing places and turning points as though conforming to some mysterious, secret ritual. There is something in the enigmatic stare of a ewe through the fence that suggests she knows perfectly well that she belongs to a flock that has been roaming these hills since prehistoric times; what's more, she knows a lot of strange and mystical things that are well outside of my comprehension. I believe her too.

It was when the sheep first started leaping over our 3-foot-6-inch boundary fence that we decided to increase its height by topping it with a concentration-camp-like barbed wire entanglement. This stopped most of them jumping over, but they were constantly roaming around the perimeter trying to find a spot where they could push under. By constant attention to our fences we managed to keep most of them out. The two exceptions were Eunice and, occasionally, her friend Harriet.

Eunice was an Olympic jumper who took our fences with remarkable efficiency and regularity. She didn't even have to run at them. One minute Eunice was standing there, outside the fence, staring purposefully into Hafod. Then suddenly she was flying into the air with the spring of a kangaroo, and landing inside the garden, with nothing to tell of her passing over the fence but a slight straggle of wool on the highest point of barbed wire. If Harriet was with her, she too would take this flying leap over the fence, but not quite so skilfully as Eunice. It was quite possible for both sheep to be munching away happily inside our fence for an hour or so before either of us spotted them. But when the cry went up 'Eunice and Harriet are in again' both Alan and I knew what to do. We had a routine performance that all of us understood. We would walk slowly towards the grazing sheep, both of whom would look up suddenly, with a pretended look of surprise on their faces. 'Goodness me,' they seemed to be saying, 'Well, well, look who's here'. 'Out!' we would say, holding aloft a pointing finger, 'Out!' Eunice and Harriet, having jumped into Hafod without any difficulty whatsoever, would pretend to be absolutely stupid when it came to finding the way out. They would make feigned jumps at impossible places, or run and butt the fence ineffectively. Sometimes they would turn round to us with looks that said, 'You don't *really* want us to go, do you?' So we decided that the least troublesome way of getting them out was to open the little gate in the fence that led from the garden into the Hafod field, and then drive them slowly towards the open gate. (We don't mind whose sheep graze the Hafod field.) We found that this system worked perfectly well. After a while Eunice and Harriet got so used to this routine that, upon seeing us advancing towards them, they would shrug their woolly shoulders and trot dutifully towards the little gate. They would occasionally stop and look round at us—just to make sure that we meant it.

There is a wealth of expression in a sheep's whole demeanour, as well as in her gaze, and we have become skilled at interpreting a sheep's behaviour. There is a man in these parts renowned for his skill in identifying a sheep by its earmark at a hundred yards distance. (I am a little suspicious of this actually. I was standing beside him once at the sheep dog trials. 'If I am reading that earmark correctly,' he said loftily, gazing across the field, 'that is Mr. Llewellyn Hughes's sheep coming in now.' He was right. But I am wondering if his reading of the shape of the ear was in any way helped by the 'Ll.H' branded on the sheep's side.) Whether or not this hundred yards identification is true, we can in fact do better than that. We can identify a sheep at *several* hundred yards distance. If there is a sheep on our ground looking guilty, then it belongs to Mr. Jones; if there is a sheep over on the Bonk (which belongs to Mr. Jones) looking guilty, then it is one of Evan Lloyd's. If there is an orderly flock of sheep munching their way across a field without the slightest intention of jumping any fences, you can bet your life they are Mr. Thomas's; and the raggle-taggle sheep in the road, getting in the way of any passing vehicles will belong to Dic and Dilwen.

Which reminds me. Dic, Dilwen and sister Gwen, together with two dogs, were visiting us on one occasion when Eunice came into the garden. We were all standing in the kitchen doorway when Dic noticed her in the wych-elm plot. 'Look,' he said, 'you've got a sheep in!' 'Never mind,' I said quickly, guessing what might be about to happen, 'don't worry, we'll get her out.' 'Oh, no, no, no,' said Dic, scrambling up the bank into the wych-elm plot, 'I will see to this for you.' He was closely followed by Dilwen, the two dogs and Gwen, who was determined to add her assistance. 'Hey-up, hey-up, hey-up!' shouted Dic, waving his stick. The dogs, instantly grasping the situation, raced across the garden. Eunice, who had never before received such treatment at Hafod, bolted towards the cottage, to be headed off by Gwen who was energetically flapping her pinafore. Doing another lap of the wych-elm plot, Eunice now made straight for the vegetable garden and cleared the fence in one easy leap, immediately followed by the two dogs and Dilwen. Charging across the beetroot and onion beds, she smashed straight through the raspberry bushes, and into the artichoke stand. There was a lot of snarling, growling and snapping of artichoke stalks as Dic leaped in amongst them flourishing his stick. Scrambling up the bank behind the artichokes and dashing between the spruce trees, the panic-stricken Eunice made a gallant attempt to charge through the perimeter fence, but only succeeded in snapping off a post and getting her head snarled up in the wire. Hemmed in now by the yelping dogs, Dic was able to grab her bodily. He heaved her up and, in one movement, threw her over the fence. He came back to us panting and beaming triumphantly. 'That got rid of the bugger,' he said.

11. Butterflies, birds and idle moments

We give names to the different areas of ground within the garden fence. The front garden, wych-elm plot, vegetable garden and woodland have already been mentioned. But there is also 'the old barn plot' (an area between the cottage and the stable from which we removed a tatty, corrugated iron hay barn and where we planted a staghorn sumach, lime, sycamore, alder and several hollies) and there is also 'whinchat patch', which lies between the vegetable garden and the Bonk, and where the whinchats come to nest each year. The piece of ground between the vegetable garden and the spring head is planted with Sitka spruce, larch and a mixture of hardwood saplings; it also supports a thriving patch of rose-bay willow-herb, and it is the flower that gives its name to this patch. 'Joe's place' is a small grass square immediately behind the cottage. It has been dug out so that it lies about four feet below the surrounding garden. It is a secret place, being entirely enclosed by sage bushes, common broom, raspberry canes and tree lupins, and the only way of getting there is by a secret winding path through some elder bushes. The square is shaded by a willow tree. Attached to the tree is an expanded poly-styrene-lined box, equipped with inside perches, which was specially designed as a wrens' winter roosting box. To our knowledge no wren has ever used it but it was a regular roosting place for a one-time Hafod great tit called Joe.

These different parts of the garden are connected by grass paths, which we try to keep neatly cut. We keep the rockeries, the front garden and—to a certain extent—the vegetable garden, free of grass and hefty weeds. This means that if we have to go away in the summer, the first job on our return is to tackle the weeds and grass that have spread to those bits of the garden we wish to keep tidy. We have now developed a routine for this work, which, given fine weather, enables us to get things looking under control again within a few days of our return. *His* first job is in the vegetable garden, wrenching out the weeds and seeing what has survived. *Her* job is to remove his piles of weeds and cart them to the compost heap. *His* job is then to sharpen and oil the grass shears and check and oil the lawn-mower. *Her* job is to use them. *His* job is to weed around the fruit bushes in the front garden. *Her* job is to pick up the weeds he has cast down upon the path that she has just that minute cut, and take them to the compost heap. And so on. (By now you have probably got the idea.) This means that in between these pockets and paths of neatness there are large patches of ground where the grass, docks, nettles, thistles, willow-herb, ragwort, knapweed and harebells grow in happy and completely uninhibited profusion. These patches belong to the Hafod wildlife, and they are strictly out of bounds during the seasons of courtship, mating, nest building, egg laying, caterpillar growing, cocoon spinning and all the other strange and mysterious things that go on in long grass, high trees and low branches throughout the spring, summer and autumn.

I don't know where all the butterflies and moths have come from. They weren't here in the beginning. A few orange-tips, meadow browns, and the tattered remains of a small tortoise-shell in an outhouse are all I can remember seeing during our first year. Now we have butterflies dancing around us through-out the summer, and we are always on the look-out for strange (to us) ones. What excitement when one of us notices a magical fluttering creature that we don't recognize! We don't know whether to stand there, drinking in all the exquisite detail of pattern, shape and colour of wing, or whether to dash indoors for the identification book, or camera, or pencil and paper. The white ermine and garden tiger moths were already known to us, but the large elephant hawk-moth had us gasping with astonishment the first time we saw one. These moths come out at dusk in June. They are beautiful. They are majestic and mysterious, their great pink wings flittering up and down across our willow-herb patch. They are with us year after year, and I don't care how much the willow-herb advances into the vegetable garden. These flowers belong to the large elephant hawk-moth, and are therefore sacred. One year we had a painted lady butterfly with us, and red admirals are now putting in an occasional appearance. Our straggling black-berries seem to have encouraged the comma butterfly; there are often two or three (of both varieties) feeding there. Little coppers are now quite numerous; they spend a lot of time twinkling around the thyme bushes. We have, of course, our fair share of cabbage whites. They plonk their eggs upon our kales and sprouts—and I pull them off again if I notice them. We aren't very bothered though. The blue tits and chaffinches, in their daily inspection of the vegetable garden, usually catch up with most of the unwanted caterpillars. The commonest butterflies at Hafod are the orange-tips, peacocks and tortoise-shells, and there are always several of them to be found in season at the springhead rockery and in the front garden.

There are plenty of cracks and crannies in our outbuildings to accommodate hibernating butterflies and moths but, given half a chance, they will come into the house. One year a per-sistent small tortoise-shell insisted upon hibernating on a bed-room ceiling. I kept putting it outside, but as soon as my back was turned it fluttered in through the open kitchen door, up the stairs and into the bedroom. In the end we let it stay. We knew that the winter temperature in our bedroom was unlikely to be high enough to disturb the tortoise-shell's slumbers. It was Christmas time before we noticed the peacock butterfly hanging upside-down from one of the parlour beams. Both butterflies stayed put throughout the winter. The small tortoise-shell woke up first. We noticed that it had started to walk around the ceiling a bit; occasionally it would tremble its wings and stretch a leg. But we didn't put it outside until the day we found it fluttering at the window. The peacock found its own way out through the door.

I have a particular affection for the small tortoise-shell butterflies. They seem to have jaunty, enquiring personalities, and I have convinced myself that there is some intelligent communication between me and them. Needless to say, I talk to *all* butterflies. ('Hey you, come on out of there,' I will scold the bedraggled, wet creature that I lift from my bucket at the spring, or 'My goodness, aren't you beautiful,' I croon over the magnificent peacock sunning itself on the ice-plant.) But from the tortoise-shell I seem to get some response. Tortoise-shells are attracted by any bright colours. They will come and examine a tin tray painted with a rose on which I sometimes carry out cups of tea into the garden; they will also come and sit upon my blouse. Once I transferred a tortoise-shell from my blouse on to my finger. Chatting to it all the while, I was able to stroke its furry back, and even uncurl its proboscis with my finger. I brought it slowly up to my face, just to see if it would look me in the eye. It put out its forelegs and plonked them on to my approaching nose, as if to say, 'Now, hang on a bit. That's quite near enough.'

Having a garden that is so far from everyone else means that I can chat to everything quite happily and without the possible embarrassment of being overheard. Trees are addressed with respect, struggling plants are given encouragement, rampaging ones are cautioned, and delicately perfumed flowers are admired. I talk to the stones, I greet the day that has just broken, dewy and fresh, and I talk to the faraway mountains. But, most of all, I talk to the birds.

The Hafod birds can be divided into three main categories. There are the summer visitors who come to nest with us each year, fussing about in the long grass and disputing each other's rights to holes in walls or ledges in outbuildings. Then there are the birds of prey, watchful and remote; and finally there are the resident garden birds who are with us all year round and who have now become part of our lives.

Springtime starts with the willow-warbler who will arrive very early one chilly April morning. His gentle song—a falling scale of sweet sadness—will penetrate my sleep-fuddled brain as I lie in bed. I struggle awake. What was that? It comes again, quietly, sadly, from somewhere over by the spruces. I pummel Alan awake. 'Willy Warble has arrived. It's spring!'

Soon the wheatears will be here, zipping up the hillside, the white badges on their backs flashing in the sun; curlews will call from the wilder places, and the cuckoo will be making a nuisance of itself everywhere. Cuckoos congregate at Hafod. In a landscape meagrely provided with trees and hedges it must be obvious to the dimmest of cuckoos that Hafod with its abundance of leafy cover is the best place in which to look for a handy nest or two in which to off-load a few eggs. They gather in the ash trees outside our bedroom window before the sun has risen on May mornings. They chortle and gurgle as well as 'cuckoo' whilst plotting the day's doings, their weird dawn chorus getting noisier and noisier. I have often stumbled crossly to the window at 3.30 or so in the morning to shake something out and drive away as many as five of them.

The planting of all these trees, shrubs, hedges and flowers at Hafod has, in fact, constituted an 'interference' in an area which was previously wide open to all the winds. This interference has meant a tremendous increase in the numbers of insects, animals and birds living here, but it has also meant a couple of losses. The swallows used to come each year to nest in the stable, but as the spring-head became enclosed with growing trees, the swallows seemed to be reluctant to drop to the water's edge to gather their mud, and when the Sitka spruce trees grew so tall that they prevented the swallows making a straightforward swoop in through the stable doorway, they stopped nesting there. They still come and visit us in the evenings. They bring their young families to practise fly-catching over the Hafod trees, and then they all sit in a line along our barbed wire fence and they chitter and twitter until darkness falls and they all have to go home. The swallows' old nests in the stable have now been taken over by wrens.

We have also lost the house-martins. They used to nest in the old corrugated iron barn that we took down (we were afraid that it was going to blow down), and they also built very insecure-looking nests high in the angle of the cottage gable-end. When we gave the cottage a coat of lime-wash the house-martins didn't like it, even though Alan made sure he left an area at the apex suitably roughened to make a reasonable 'key' for house-martin mud. They kept on flying up there, clinging to the wall for a while, chittering and discussing the matter between themselves; but they didn't like it. And they have never nested there since.

The birds of prey sometimes present us with a few problems. We love to hear their music; the 'mew' of a buzzard, and the high 'keeuw' of the kestrel are background sounds to our lives. We know that they have to eat small birds and rob nests, but we wish they wouldn't come after ours. When a hungry kestrel comes hunting over the Hafod trees, pandemonium will break out. The air will be strident with a chorus of frightened chitterings, chinkings, cluckings and tickings as birds race for cover beneath the spruce trees or into the thickest hedge. Once when we came back from a trip away to find that a kestrel had actually taken to roosting upon our bedroom window-sill we just didn't know what to do. It was obvious, from the pile of droppings and pellets, that he had been using the sill for quite some time. It was also obvious that the sill was, so far as he was concerned, a very comfortable and satisfactory place to sleep. With the chaffinches and mistle thrushes nesting nearby, he could very nearly have breakfast in bed! But he looked so pretty and cosy snuggled down in the corner that we didn't have the heart to disturb him. We made sure that the bedroom curtains were pulled across well before roosting time so that we shouldn't upset him when we went to bed. When we were reasonably sure that he was asleep we would peep out at him— a neat ball of brown feathers and fluff. He was a restless sleeper (probably dreaming of all those high-speed hunts) and frequently during the night he would shuffle around and shake his head, so that his beak rattled against the glass. To think of this strange and wild bird snoozing away only a few inches from my head made me curiously happy. When spring came 'Kezzy' took himself off to raise a family—presumably in the old quarry nearby—and he didn't return until late autumn. He sleeps at Hafod only occasionally now, although we often see him hunting over our field and garden.

Magpies are clowns. Bouncing about the hillside on india-rubber legs and cackling like hens, they make us laugh. But they don't amuse our nesting birds, who cry out in alarm when the magpie comes amongst them. One year the magpies had the audacity to make a nest seven feet off the ground in a Sitka spruce. It was a ridiculous great twiggy thing, almost the size of my linen basket, and hanging out on all sides of the spruce tree. Just the sort of nest you would expect from such clowns. Once again we were in a dilemma. If we let the magpies stay, what about all our other nesting birds? Again the situation was saved by our doing nothing and letting nature take its course. Our resident crows (who nest each year in the old rowan tree upon the hillside) weren't going to allow the magpies to nest so close to crow territory and, after a few mid-air battles and a lot of magpie-versus-crow swearing matches, the magpies took themselves off and nested elsewhere. But their crazy nest in the spruce tree is still with us.

One Boxing Day I tossed out into the field the carcass of our Christmas chicken so that any passing animal might finish it off. We were rewarded with the sight of a magpie and one of our feral cats feeding together quite peacefully. Were they sinking their differences for the season of goodwill?

Most people can understand why we are so busy at Hafod during the spring, summer and autumn—what with all that vegetable growing, fruit picking, jam making, grass cutting and Christmas tree clearing—but we sometimes get the puzzled question of what on earth we do in winter. If it so happens that we are not away from home during the winter months then it is possible for us to spend weeks on end at Hafod, sometimes completely cut off from the outside world in a snow-covered landscape which the sun rises to touch at about 9.00 a.m. but which is left in gathering darkness by about 4.00 p.m. What do we do? We just, well, *live*.

Hafod, in mid-winter, on a sunlit, snowy morning has a fragile, quiet feeling. The latch on the kitchen door snaps open with a loud intrusive click, and there is this great breathless hush out of doors. The wide stretch of snow-locked moorland, with the mountains behind thrusting icy peaks to the sky, looks so fantastic, so awe-inspiring, so moving, that I feel there should be a great blast of music, a great triumphant chord of proclamation. But there is nothing. Nothing but an immense white silence. And I don't know whether to burst into tears, or dance in the snow.

But close at hand there *are* sounds. Little sounds, like the tinkling plop of a small icicle dripping into a hole in the snow; a dry wind gently crackling in the twigs of the ash trees; the faint murmur of the spring water moving over the cold stone waterfalls, and a little, snow-scattering flutter in the spruce trees as a bird comes to be fed. Of course! *That's* what we do in winter! We feed the birds!

Our resident garden birds are blue and great tits, chaffinches, blackbirds, dunnocks, mistle thrushes and robins, and they *all* demand to be fed. I haven't included the wrens in this list. Wrens are long-standing Hafod residents but they survive the winter months by some mysterious means known only to wrens. I have never known a wren take any food that we have offered. We have two main feeding stations (to avoid quarrelling). One is near the back door on a marble-topped stone wall (where I stand my summer wash tub), and the other is a triangular, plastic sink tidy, clipped (for easy removal) to a wooden frame attached to the kitchen window. The first job on a winter's morning is to clear the snow from the marble slab and the sink tidy. The marble slab will be given a scattering of oatmeal, suet, currants and any stale breadcrumbs; the sink tidy will be filled with a hunk of cheese rind or a lump of fat or old bone. This lot will keep many of the birds happy for quite some time, but we have a few who demand individual attention. No eating oatmeal with the masses for them; they are entitled to be hand-fed, with peanuts. Sometimes I pretend that I am not going to co-operate. 'There's enough here for everyone,' I say, and I come into the kitchen and shut the door. They will fly to the window-sill and line up angrily—an indignant congregation of great and blue tits. If I move to the wash-up corner, they will fly around the house to face me accusingly through the window.

We once had a blue tit called Pip, who, having discovered that the kitchen was the source of all food, endeavoured to stay inside the house for as long as possible. He even tried to roost with us—a practice that we didn't encourage. It wasn't that we objected to this little ball of fluff perching underneath the lampshade, or upon the curtain rail, but we were always fearful that a bird left alone in the kitchen might injure itself upon the stove. A roosting bird might be awake and searching for food long before we were stirring in the morning, and the thought of those tiny feet possibly landing unwittingly upon the hot-plate was just too horrifying. If Pip was flying around the kitchen at dusk we shooed him out. But one night we missed him. We had looked in all his usual would-be kitchen roosting places and, not finding him, assumed he was in the garden. We went to bed, leaving our clothes lying on our kitchen chairs, and when I came down in the morning I was astonished to see a sleepy-looking Pip snuggled up comfortably inside Alan's vest. (Pip was a particular friend of his. The brim of Alan's hat hanging in the kitchen was one of Pip's perching places, and he also occasionally clung to his beard, searching for crumbs. Sometimes he found them.) Pip extracted himself from the folds of the vest, stretched a wing and a leg, and then hopped on to the back of the chair. He then sat there, watching me go about my morning tasks. I riddled the stove, and put the kettle on to the hot-plate. I helped myself to hot water from the stove's side-tank, washed myself and dressed. 'You naughty bird,' I scolded him, 'where on earth were you hiding last night?' He wasn't telling. He just sat there, carefully watching me.

When I went to the shelf and reached down the jar of oatmeal, Pip was instantly alert and ready for action. By this time a line of hungry faces was at the kitchen window and Pip, obviously wishing to demonstrate his superior position, flew across to the window-ledge and peered out at them. 'Yah, boo!' he seemed to say. The expressions of astonishment and fury on the faces of his mates must have afforded him great satisfaction. But he didn't enjoy his gleeful triumph for long. Marching outside with the jar of oatmeal, I closed the door upon Pip in the kitchen and scattered the food liberally along the window-sill in front of his greedy eyes. A cluster of great and blue tits and chaffinches immediately came to feed, leaving a furious little Pip, bouncing up and down with rage on the other side of the glass. I waited until almost all the food was gone before I let him out.

But the birds don't come to us solely for food. Sometimes they come just to be friendly. The kitchen door is normally wide open, except during the cold and wet weather, and in order to keep out any wandering mouse the doorway is guarded at the base by a 9-inch-high piece of wood. Scrit, our blackbird, likes to sit upon this piece of wood and sing quiet little sub-songs. He will sit there singing to himself quite happily so long as I am clattering about in the kitchen. If I stop working, or go and speak to him, he will instantly stop singing and look self-conscious. Sometimes, on these occasions, I toss him a scrap of food. He looks down at it with one eye, half-heartedly, and more often than not he will ignore it and carry on warbling to himself as soon as my back is turned.

When Alan is working around the garden he will always have a personal attendant of some bird or another. I once went to look for him and found him sitting happily in the privy, the door open to the sunshine and the view. With his trousers around his ankles he was enjoying a quiet smoke. A few inches further along the pine-wood seat sat an equally contented-looking blue tit. On another occasion I went to fetch him for coffee and found him hammering out some copper sheet in the outhouse. He was making a lot of dust and a lot of noise; and he was completely oblivious of the fact that, only a few feet away from him, Pinny was sitting in a patch of sunshine on an old sack, just watching him. Chaffinches are also fond of him. He had an affair with a female chaffinch (known as Miss Chee) which lasted for several years. She used to follow him around. One day he spent some hours shifting a load of coal that had been dumped in the field. With his wheelbarrow he trudged back and forth between the field and the chicken house (where we kept the coal then). Walking behind him—a few feet away

—was Miss Chee. Hopping over the tussocks of grass, walking daintily where the grass was short, she trailed behind him like a little shadow all morning.

We seem to communicate with our birds on two levels. There is the chatty, cheerful level with the birds we know personally; they can tell what we are thinking because of the tone of our voices and our actions. In the same way we are able to know what they want. But there is also a deeper, more urgent, form of communication, usually in times of distress, and quite often with birds that would normally keep their distance from us. One year the pair of swallows that were nesting in the stable came to the cottage door. They hovered in the doorway chittering with anxiety, then flew back to the stable. Within seconds they were back again, hovering and crying. The message was loud and clear. Please come and help! We raced along to the stable, and found a cat standing on top of one of the wooden partitions, almost within a paw's reach of the nest of youngsters peering anxiously over the edge. On another occasion Alan was able to communicate to a frightened robin a sensible course of action. The Hafod robins are now happy, friendly little chaps, but in the early days they were very timid. This particular robin (called Isaac) flew into the kitchen by accident one day. Panic-stricken, he fluttered first of all at the kitchen window, and then shot up the stairs. He flew crazily around a large cupboard off the landing when Alan went up, and he battered himself against the skylight in a frenzy. Alan walked across to Isaac, holding out his hand, and saying 'Come on, robin'. He said he felt *strongly* that the robin *must* sit upon his hand. And he did. He stayed absolutely still as Alan approached with an outstretched hand until his fingers were at his breast; then Isaac lightly stepped on. Alan carried him to the window in the nearest bedroom, opened it, and a very frightened Isaac was free.

But sometimes we haven't been able to help the birds. One year our blackbird and several chaffinches died. We suspect that they had been eating 'dressed' rape seed. In the evening of their death the chaffinches were coming to us; hopping unsteadily across the kitchen floor, looking up at us, begging us to *do* something to help. We could do nothing for any of them other than to make their last hours as comfortable as we knew how. We don't seem to have been much help to injured birds either. We have read of marvellous people who make splints for birds with broken legs or wings, and nurse them back to full strength. We are always reluctant to handle a bird in case, in our clumsiness, we make matters worse. For a couple of years a one-legged female great tit (called, of course, Peggy) was able to survive at Hafod, and we like to think that our plastic sink tidy feeding-tray kept her going in the winter. It was noticeable that, whereas she couldn't stand to feed on the marble slab, she was able to squat in the sink tidy and eat all she wanted.

I rely on some form of instinct to tell me when and when not to handle a bird. I had no doubts about taking hold of the swallow I found in difficulties in the stable. This bird had been ringed and the leg bearing the ring had become tangled up with a roll of thin wire hanging over a nail in the stable. I disentangled the swallow and took it outside to have a look at the leg. It appeared to be uninjured, and the offending ring was slightly open. I prised it off, and let it drop into the grass, and the swallow flew off with a few happy swoops. (I removed the coil of wire to a safe place.) I don't know whether this particular swallow nested with us that season or not. Where swallows nest, where they go, and which way they travel is their business. It's nothing to do with me.

I am not at all happy about this custom of clamping rings to birds' legs. Certainly it is interesting to know that a bird ringed at Observatory X flies to Africa via Observatory Y, but surely we are not entitled to gain this information at the expense of a bird's comfort and perhaps even its life? How many seabirds have died lonely deaths, with ringed feet entangled in seaweed, I wonder? How many tiny willow-warblers taking that long and exhausting flight across the seas find that the extra weight of a ring on their leg is the last straw that sends them plummeting down into the waves? How many birds are injured in the traps set by these ring-happy ornithologists? All the information we gain regarding a bird's movements between continents . . . what good does this knowledge do the bird? There are a lot of questions to be asked about the ringing of birds, and I wish the whole business could be stopped until a few satisfactory answers have been provided.

Which brings me to the ringed pigeon who dropped in to see us one day. 'Dropped' is absolutely the right word here. Poor pigeon literally fell out of the sky. I think he was trying to perch upon the ash tree but, exhausted and soaking wet, he simply fell through the branches and lay on the ground at the base of the tree. It was a wild November evening and if I hadn't actually been looking out of the window at the time, he would probably have stayed there in the driving rain all night. We carried him into the chicken house and placed him in a shallow, sack-lined basket. We put some oatmeal and currants there with him, and a dish of water, and left him. The next day we found him exactly as we had left him. He stared at us blearily, and didn't attempt to move away. The food and water were untouched. Guessing that he was used to special pigeon food, I cycled to Llanrwst to buy some—but found that no shop stocked such food. They don't go in for pigeon fancying around here. I saw Muriel in the car park and told her my problem. Could she suggest what else the pigeon might eat? She couldn't. So I cycled home again, wondering how we were going to persuade our guest to change his diet. We needn't have worried. Later that evening, Muriel staggered up the path carrying a 7-lb bag of pigeon food. 'Managed to get it in Colwyn Bay,' she said. We threw away the rejected currants and oatmeal and offered our pigeon a dish of mixture from Muriel's 7-lb bag. He wasn't interested. He just sat there looking at us. On the second day when we went into the chicken house in the morning the pigeon (whom we now called Henry) wasn't in his basket; he was sitting on top of an old sweeping brush that was up-ended against one of the walls. He appeared to have taken some of the food. So we left some more food there and wedged the door open.

During the next few days Henry explored Hafod. He would
fly up to the stable roof, then to the cottage roof, and occasionally potter about on the lawn and around the paths. He returned each evening to the chicken house to feed and to roost
on the old brush. We knew that we were supposed to make a
note of Henry's ring numbers and notify the police who would
contact the owner to make arrangements for the bird's collection. It all seemed a lot of fuss and bother, so we decided to let
Henry choose for himself. So long as he wanted to stay, we
would feed and shelter him. But he was free to go. One day he
flew off for several hours and we thought he had left us. But,
when evening came, he was back there up on the stable roof,
waiting to drop down for his supper and bed. Sometimes he
went missing for a couple of days and then returned. Finally he
disappeared altogether. We guess that he was increasing his
distances each day and 'feeling out' the right direction for
home. Anyway, we loved having him . . . and we've still got
half a jar of Muriel's pigeon food left if ever he is passing this
way again.

12. The water garden

Hafod's water supply is a spring that gushes (or trickles, according to the weather) out of the ground at the base of the hill. Sometimes furious, sometimes meek, but always endearing, our spring is known to us as 'Minnie', and when we first set eyes on her we decided that she was worthy of a better setting than a muddy hole in a bank. But the transformation of Minnie took place gradually, over the next few years.

In order to make it easier to collect water in a bucket, someone once shoved a glazed drain-pipe into the hillside, and most of the water now flows through this pipe. It is possible to peer up the pipe and see the water running over solid rock, and at one time we toyed with the idea of digging back to this rock so that the spring head might be made into a more attractive place. But we had heard that springs were temperamental things and, if interfered with, our spring might take umbrage and disappear underground. So we decided to leave it alone and, instead, to build around the drain-pipe with additional rocks. But this wasn't the first improvement; there were other aspects of the water garden to consider. The whole area was going to change gradually.

The spring water used to run from the pipe straight down a narrow, stony bed and into a pond near the roadside wall. When the spring ran slowly this bed was often dry and so could support no form of life. When we fenced off the spring to include it into our garden area we took the fence across the stream-bed just above the pond, so that animals grazing in the field would still have access to water. Alan then got to work on that featureless, stony bed. By widening the bed in some places, deepening it in other places, introducing wide, level rock ledges and narrow gullies, he created a stream-bed where water gathered in pools, then tumbled over little waterfalls. This meant that even when the spring was running very slowly there were always pools of water all the way down the slope.

The obvious crossing place of this streamlet was at the top near the spring. You simply walked down a muddy slope, stepped across the water, and scrambled up another muddy slope on the other side. As 'muddy slopes' didn't feature in Alan's scheme of things, he set about changing it. He dug away the banks; altered the course of the water slightly; added a few rocks; created another pool and generally messed about until the final shape materialized. He made a level approach to the stream on both sides and, with two long and massive stones (moved with the aid of a friend), he constructed a mini clapper bridge,* which he covered with turf. We can now walk on a level, winding, grass path from the spring path, over the clapper bridge and into the bluebell wood.

We dedicated our spring to the naiad of our stream (we call her Araneida)—and started to plant flowers. Saxifrage and stonecrops were invited to take a grasp of the soil in between the rocks, then various primulas, daffodils and the pretty, scented creeping toadflax were introduced. Ice-plants, London pride and cotton lavender now tumble and cling to the spring side, with golden-rod, red-hot poker, tansy and Michaelmas daisies peeping from behind.

Then we had a bonus. We were working early one spring at a large country house in Derbyshire where one of Alan's jobs was to help clear out a Victorian bog garden because the ground was wanted for a tennis court. He was invited to help himself to any plants. We returned to Hafod with a van full of strange rhizomes, roots and cuttings, and the spring side has never looked the same since.

We have now forgotten the proper names of some of these plants. There is one that comes thrusting up through the soil each year that we call the 'umbrella plant' or the 'water carrier'. In early spring its flowers appear like deep pink lilies of the valley. Later come the large leaves, shaped something like convolvulus flowers, and these leaves always contain water,

* A common West Country name for a simple stone-slab bridge.

even during dry periods, because the overnight dew runs down
the sides and collects in the bottom. Then there are the giant
hogweeds (*Heracleum mantegazzianum*). We are delighted with
these great pantomime plants—and they seem to be delighted
with Hafod, because they are seeding themselves all over the
place. Sometimes reaching eight feet high, they often have a
dozen or so large heads the size of meat plates, much to the
delight of the birds who feast upon the seeds in the autumn. I
suppose our most striking plant is the gunnera (*Gunnera chilensis*
or *scabra*). This waterside monster has exceeded our expecta-
tions. An exposed moorland 1,000 feet above sea-level seems
hardly the place to grow a gunnera. But ours didn't know that
and it is now spreading at a fantastic rate, sending out great,
fiery-red flower spikes the size of coal hods, and covering a wide
area with leaves that are often five foot across. Dic and Dilwen
are horrified by it. Such a monstrous-looking plant must surely
be poisonous, they think. They look at the prickly stems with
great suspicion, and give the whole plant a wide berth. They
call it the 'Hafod rhubarb'. When the young man on the
library van heard that we were growing a gunnera he asked if
he could have a bit of the root for the stream side in his garden.
Alan said that he certainly could, and the following fortnight
when the van called at the village Alan took him down 'a bit of
root'. The librarian was expecting to receive something in a
polythene bag he could carry home on the bus. He was rather
taken aback when Alan staggered through the door carrying a
massive muddy hunk in a 2-foot-square cardboard box. But,
looking at our gunnera, you couldn't see where this 'bit of
root' had been taken from.

With the water garden now becoming lush with shady greenery, and scented with sweet flowers, we noticed that other
things were beginning to happen. Just above the bottom pond,
and inside the garden fence, Alan had formed a deeper pool in
a roughly kidney shape, with a little stone causeway across the
centre. The gunnera stood as king over this pool, but the banks
were also planted with various mints, purple loosestrife, mont-
bretia, daffodils, primroses, Rodger's bronze leaf (*Rodgersia*

podophylla), hostas, saxifrages, polygonums, goatsbeards and Russian comfrey. 'This,' said Alan, 'would be a nice place for frogs.' Obviously the frogs thought so too because, before long, we noticed that frog spawn was filling the pool. Then other creatures began to appear in the smaller pools upstream. Water beetles scooted around in the depths of the water, and little spiders danced across its surface. There were so many things to watch and look for we seemed to be spending a lot of time at the spring. So Alan began to build seats into his spring side rockery —which meant more excavations, more rocks and boulders, and more saxifrages and stonecrops. Now there is so much going on it is difficult to decide which seat to take. If you sit on the right of the spring you can watch the tiny frogs clambering in and out of the stones at the springhead, or you can look across to the bluebell wood. On the other hand, if you sit the other side of the spring you can look downstream and see the birds come to drink or bathe in the pools, or lark about with each other underneath the gunnera leaves. Once we watched a battle between a frog and a water shrew. We were glad that the frog got away by leaping downstream. The shrew, squeaking with frustration, danced around a bit on one of the waterfall ledges, and then darted back to his hole in the bank.

I surprised a wren at the springhead one day. I came round the corner in the path to find him standing upon our bucket having a drink. He took off suddenly and flew straight up Minnie. He obviously found it cool, damp and interesting up there because I had to stand for several minutes in the bluebell wood waiting for him to reappear at the spring mouth again. There is a family of bank voles living in the rockery behind the springhead. We often see one of them, with a mouthful of nest material or food, diving underneath a clump of saxifrage into a hole between the stones. We have watched bank voles coming and going to and from this hole for several years and we think that they are all descendants of the original pair because they always follow the same complicated route to the old family home. They often forage around near the main pond and then make for home up the side of the stream. They nip behind a large upright stone, scurry across the main spring path and dive into a conduit that was constructed as a frog 'escape route'. From here they work their way up between the stones forming one of the seats, and across the back of another seat, making a final dash across the marble slab on top of the spring, and then into the saxifrage. Such a carefully worked out trail must surely have been shown by mother to offspring all down the generations.

Alan likes humping rocks about. If he finds a rock of some significance—because of its shape or colour or feel—then it has to be placed in a significant position. And seeing some of the things he has done with rocks at Hafod makes me wonder if those chaps at Stonehenge were just enjoying themselves, like Alan. He was moving a large, rounded stone once into a position at the 'toe' of the elder plantation near the back door, when it occurred to him that the day on which he was doing this work was the day before his fortieth birthday. The stone has always since been referred to as his '39th stone'. When that particular anniversary came along for me, another suitable stone was found (this time a tall, pointed one) and, with due ceremony, I helped to hump it into another significant position (at the end of the spring path).

Alan gives a lot of thought to the positioning of stones, and he usually manages to line them up with other features which he considers to be significant. For example, I am told that one particular stone is on a 'ley' passing through a mound on the moors behind us, a skyline notch and a ford on the old drovers' road, an ancient crossroads, two cairns and nineteen other natural and man-made features. We have another stone that is direct in line between the midsummer sunset over the Carneddau, an oak tree he planted in the field, and the wych-elm (which is also on the previously mentioned ley). He was rolling a stone into position one day when Muriel was visiting us. 'Why are you putting that stone there?' she demanded. 'Well', said Alan sarcastically, 'if you look carefully, you will see that this stone is on a direct ley between Mr. Lloyd's gate-post, the patch of rhubarb and the privy door handle.' 'Oh, you should have seen a programme on television last week,' said Muriel (she is always telling us of programmes we should have seen on television). 'It was all about leys and that sort of thing.' 'I bought a book on the subject, years ago,' replied Alan, 'It was written by Alfred Watkins, the photographer.' 'This programme,' went on Muriel, 'explained all about it. These leys are supposed to be lines of force across the country.' 'Watkins didn't claim that,' said Alan, 'and I prefer *his* inter- pretation.' 'They are marked by pine trees and things,' Muriel insisted, 'and certain stones at high points . . . or was it low points? You really should have seen the programme; it would have told you all about it.' 'But I have the book by Alfred Watkins!' Alan was nearly shouting now, 'And it's fully illus- trated with typical leys and mark points.' 'Well, it was a very interesting programme,' Muriel concluded, 'and I think it was somebody called Watson, or Wilkins, who developed the theory.'

I wonder if Alan's stones will be standing upon this hillside in a few thousand years' time? And will some learned people attribute obscure geometrical, numerical, philosophic, re- ligious or astronomic reasons to their positions? Whatever carefully worked-out conclusions they come to, I bet they never discover which is *his* 39th stone, or *her* 39th stone!

As I walk around the garden, the stones evoke different re- sponses from me. This one, perhaps, asks to be sat upon for a moment; that one I just stand and look at; another one I must touch when passing. There is a pleasing and harmonious re- lationship between the cold, solid permanence of the stones, the warm but temporary presence of me, and the transient fragility of delicate flowers, like this Welsh poppy, whose petals may fall in a day.

We have a perpetual feeling of wonder and astonishment here. As well as the mysteries of things that are living and growing, there are strange occurrences that we do not under- stand but have come to accept. There is a small whirlwind that visits us every now and then. It appears during differing weather conditions and seasons, but it always starts in the same way. There will be a high whistling sound coming from the top of the Bonk. We look up to see the bracken moving around up there. Then this small area of movement (a few feet in diameter) will travel down the hillside in the direction of the spring. It will cross the springhead, cut through the woodland and vanish across the moor. It is not violent; it just sends all the foliage swishing about in a circular motion. All the time there is this high-pitched whistling. We have another high-pitched singing noise that we hear amongst the trees sometimes. This has occurred only during calm, dry weather. When I first heard it I thought it was a far-away vehicle approaching, or the sound of some machinery operating in a distant farm. I drew Alan's attention to it. Then we discovered that we heard it only when we stood in certain spaces between our blocks of trees. We lost the sound immediately we moved out into the open. It was a clear, high-pitched, unvarying humming sound. Not very loud, not disturbing, nor particularly attractive. It was just there. I think our senses are particularly receptive here, and we will 'home-in' on any sensitive atmosphere.

We feel this more particularly in our relationship with the living things at Hafod. We are convinced that anything that has life will respond to love. Take the wych-elm, for instance. We have some photographs of the wych-elm that we took before we moved here. One photograph is of the front of the cottage; the wych-elm happens to be in the background. It is not a very large tree, as wych-elms go (probably about a hundred and fifty years old), and in this winter snapshot it looks rather thin and tired. It was only when we were comparing this photograph with a recent one taken at a similar angle and at a similar time of year that we realized the wych-elm had changed. The whole tree appears to be sturdier and stronger and happier. And what have we done for the wych-elm? Nothing, except love it.

We love the two old ash trees in front of the cottage too. But they used to worry us. Standing about seventy feet high, and towering over the cottage, they roared with a frightening frenzy when a gale was blowing. We used to cower beneath the bed-clothes during storm-lashed nights, hoping that the gods would protect us. We knew that we ought to have the trees topped or felled. But they stood between the shippen, the stable, the cottage and the road. It would be an awkward and expensive job. What's more we didn't really want to lose them. So we just kept delaying the decision. Then one day the ash trees gave us a warning. The wind during the night had not been particularly strong, and we had heard no unusual noises to worry us. But in the morning we found that a very large and heavy bough had fallen from one of the trees. This bough had partially overhung the cottage. How it fell to earth without striking the cottage we do not know; but there it was, across the lawn, as though neatly laid out for our inspection. 'Please *do* something about us,' the ash trees were saying, 'we can't guarantee not to hit you next time.' So we did. What's more, the whole performance was not such a bother as we had imagined it would be. We found an excellent firm of tree fellers who made a very neat job of topping and trimming the two trees to a height of about twenty feet. The trees have since sprouted out with renewed vigour, and have reclothed themselves with a great green twiggy fuzz. They are now a delight to the mistle thrushes and blackbirds who roost in them, and to the tits, tree creepers and wrens who clamber about their crusty old trunks in search of food.

'I like it here,' Dic said recently, 'it's so, so sort of *quiet*.' This, coming from a man who lives in a spot even more isolated than we do is astonishing. But I don't really think he meant that it was 'quiet'. He had sensed a difference between the feeling at Hafod, and the feeling at his farm, but was unable to find the right words. Possibly he could have expressed himself better in Welsh.

If there is one place above all others within the garden that holds the spirit of Hafod, it is at the spring. It is to the spring we go with our first cups of coffee in the morning, and usually with our elevenses and our afternoon tea. It is to the spring we go first when we return after a period of absence, and it is at the spring we end our evening walks around the garden. If I have letters to write, peas to shell, or thoughts to think, it is to the spring that I take them. On hot summer evenings we have shower baths at the spring—larking about with a watering-can in the privacy of our woodland. When we need a haircut we carry chair, scissors and comb along to the spring, unless the weather is cold or wet.

Neither of us has been to a hairdresser now for about seventeen years and we have become quite skilled at cutting each other's hair when necessary. Our hair seems to grow at similar rates and so we reach a certain undesirable state of shagginess at the same time. Having one's hair cut is quite a drowsy, soothing pastime, and if it can be carried out in the happy surroundings near the spring, so much the better. Alan usually does mine first. I settle down comfortably in the chair, my head cocked down at an angle that sends my gaze into the top spring pool. I can see a frog at the side of the pool, partially concealed by a leaf of monkey flower. Some of the water spiders are fighting over the corpse of a fly tangled up in the crowfoot. Other spiders lie motionless in a line along a stone face. (Alan has arranged all these stones with great care, taking into account not only the pleasant surfaces we want to look at and the useful shapes for channelling water, but also the crevices, passage ways and miniature caverns that must be created for the use of frogs, voles, and any passing water sprite.) There is a sudden ripple from underneath the clapper bridge. I think another frog is there. I lapse into a sort of dreamy doze whilst I wait for the clapper bridge frog to appear. Then Alan jabs me awake. 'Get up, I want you to turn round the other way now.' We shuffle around, and I am now facing the woodland. I am looking straight ahead at a clump of mountain blewetts. It is a rather shaggy, untidy plant but the closed flower buds appear to be enclosed in a delicate diamond pattern net. It is the black frilly edges of the green bracts which make the net pattern; these bracts clothe the bud like the breast feathers of a tiny bird. The buds must have some sticky sweetness about them; I notice that a lot of flies and several wasps are clambering over the buds whilst ignoring the bright blue, open flowers. I hardly have two seconds, it seems, to reflect upon this interesting fact when Alan is poking me again to say that my hair is done, and

it's his turn now. We change places. Now I must concentrate
upon what I am doing. Alan's hair is thick and unruly. He
doesn't demand a 'short-back-and-sides' cut, but he likes it
neatly tapered at the back. Then there is that difficult bit over
the ear. I must try to get a nice arch there. Unfortunately he
seems to be dozing off, and I have to keep on yanking his head
around. Funny how he seems to have a thicker bunch of hair
over one ear. I must snip off all those odd straggly hairs between
his hair-line and his beard. 'I've just noticed an interesting
thing,' Alan says dreamily, 'those mountain blewetts—they
must have sticky buds. See how they are covered with flies and
wasps. . . .'

13. The drought

We thought we knew all about the North Wales climate. The weather pattern used to be something like this—The division between winter and summer called 'spring' was not easy to recognize. March and April were normally cold and dry, and any precipitation quite often fell in the form of snow. These months were usually also very windy, and the cold, dry winds held back seed germination. Then, quite suddenly in May, there would be almost an explosion of sunshine and warmth. It was possible for us to be working one day all muffled up in vests and pullovers, then to be stripped down to shorts and shirts the next day. June and July would be the glorious summer months; August would often be cool and wet. September was usually mild and sunny, and we were sometimes lucky with a warm October. Then, in November, winter would be breathing down our necks again, but the heavy snows didn't usually come until January or February.

We were frequently cut off by the snow in those early days. It wasn't the quantity of falling snow that caused the trouble, but the blizzards that threw the snow around in gigantic drifts of fantastic shapes. It was sometimes possible to walk to the village across comparatively snow-free fields, whereas the road was impassable and filled to the wall top with snow. We never minded being cut off from the rest of the world. There was always plenty of food in store. Digging a path to the spring was fun, and carrying out our daily tasks under difficult conditions presented a challenge to which we responded gleefully. If the windcharger had frozen in the furled position we might decide to leave it furled (and manage on paraffin lighting if the batteries were not fully charged) or we might decide to make an expedition up the hill with the ladder to see if we could free the tail vane. The decision would depend upon just how much

snow was lying on the hill, and whether or not the day was
bright and sunny. Floundering around in knee-high drifts
whilst carrying a ladder can be a hilarious lark in sun-sparkling
snow under a bright blue sky. But if a blizzard were raging and
visibility practically nil, we would probably decide that such a
trip would be a pointless struggle as we might have to battle up
the slope again later in the day if the wind increased in strength
and the windcharger needed furling again. The wind would
sculpt artistic snowdrifts across our hillside. Creamy waves
with delicately tapering tops looped up the side of the Bonk.
The tips of these snowdrifts were constantly changing shape as
spindrift blew like spirals of smoke away from their edges.

Northwesterly and southwesterly gales can hit us at any time
of the year. Storm-force winds are common here, and gusts to
hurricane force not unusual.

But during the past five or six years the weather seems to have
changed. We have not had a severe winter. We have been in the
surprising position of looking from the kitchen window on to a
lightly snow-covered moor, listening to tales on the radio of
people in South Wales, Devon and Cornwall dying in snowdrifts. Also, there hasn't been so much rain. Flooding in the
Conwy valley used to be a regular, twice-yearly occurrence. It
hasn't happened so often nor to such an extent during the past
few years.

We observed these changes with an academic interest only.
Whatever weather came our way we would cope. The garden
was now sheltered from the worst of the wind; our drainage
channels were always kept free in case of flood. The weather
could do what it liked; we should survive. We thought we knew
all the answers. That was until the summer of 1976.

At first we were sitting pretty. Our radio informed us that
the rest of the country was in the grip of a severe drought. Stand
pipes were being erected in city streets, and there was talk of
water rationing. But at Hafod we were enjoying one of the best
summers we had ever known. For the first time the springtime
had been *warm*. We seemed to be having normal amounts of
rain, so our vegetable seeds were germinating and developing

at an unbelievable rate. Occasional light rain continued to fall in May and the first part of June. A couple of weeks went by without rain, and it was noticeable that Minnie was sending down less water. We weren't worried. Our spring had been much lower than this on many previous occasions and, according to local people, it was totally reliable. Within living memory the spring at Hafod had never been known to dry up in summer nor to freeze in winter.

By the end of July Minnie was very low indeed. It was now taking half an hour for a bucket to fill with water. The bottom (field) pond was dry and the main pond was diminishing. When Alan created this pond he dug out a small area on one side extra deep so that even in dry weather there would always be a deep pool for the tadpoles. Now that the water was falling it was noticeable how overcrowded with tadpoles the pools seemed to be. But the weather was still not worrying us. We had been through all these extremes before, and the garden had got off to such a good start that we foresaw no difficulties there. We were having marvellous pickings of seakale beet. We had never seen such large leaves before. In spite of the continued dry weather everything looked lush and green. Collecting water for the house was an all-day job, but it didn't matter. I just left a bucket at the spring, and changed it every time I happened to be passing.

August came in dry and hot. Day after day the sun poured down on us from a brilliant blue sky. We pottered around our daily tasks wearing nothing, or next to nothing. Alan's tan gradually changed from a light mud colour to a rich mahogany. The heat was never unpleasant. The spruce trees and cypresses threw a dark-green, cool shade along the spring path, and the woodland air was light with dappled shade, but I must admit that we didn't sit so long at Minnie. There are no trees immediately overhanging the springhead and by mid-morning the stones were so hot to the touch that it was not at all comfortable for naked thighs.

We were starting to worry about the tadpoles. The household bucket was now spending so long underneath the trickle of spring water that very little was running down the stream-bed. The pools were getting lower. The soil in the vegetable garden was now looking desert-dry and there were a few plants in the front garden showing signs of suffering. I started to save my washing-up water and I carried it down to pour over a little chestnut tree that was visibly wilting, or I gave it to the banks of thyme and sage.

Then we heard that our neighbour's spring had dried up. Mr. Jones has water brought into his house from a tank in the field which is fed by a good spring. But one day when Mrs. Jones turned on the tap there was no water. Investigation of the tank found that it was completely dry. The spring had stopped running. Mr. and Mrs. Jones were not in danger of dying of thirst because their son, who has a mains water supply at his house, travelled across to his parents' farm each day bringing churns of water to fill up the tank. So their situation, although difficult, was not desperate. But the news of their water failure was something of a shock to us. Their spring also had the reputation of never drying up. For the first time that summer a gnawing worry started to trouble me. Just supposing . . . what if the unbelievable happened . . . what would we do if . . .? No. It couldn't possibly happen! Minnie was magical! Minnie was under the care of Araneida, our naiad. Minnie couldn't possibly dry up! . . . Could she?

We started to keep a record of the time the bucket was taking to fill:

Tuesday, 17 August — Minnie's morning bucket: 38 minutes

Wednesday, 18 August — Minnie's morning bucket: $41\frac{1}{2}$ minutes

Thursday, 19 August — Minnie's morning bucket: 45 minutes

It was noticeable that the last bucket of the day took considerably longer to fill than the first bucket, and that Minnie seemed to refresh herself somewhat overnight. For example, the bucket I collected from her during the evening of Thursday, 19 August, took *1 hour 14 minutes* to fill. But the next morning, Friday, 20

August, the bucket filled in $48\frac{1}{2}$ minutes. But the overall pattern was depressingly obvious. Minnie was getting slower and slower each day.

'I'm worried about you,' my mother wrote. 'The reservoirs are very low here and we are all having to save water. How are you managing?' I wrote back a bright, reassuring letter. 'Don't worry, Mum. Our spring has never been known to dry up and, anyway, if it does,' . . . (the faintest of doubts were now beginning to creep up on me) . . . 'we shall simply take our buckets down to the river.'

The 'river' is a broad stream which flows strongly through a small valley that lies between us and the village. It is about a quarter of a mile away from us, and fetching water from there in buckets would be a wearisome, but perfectly feasible, task. If necessary we could do this, but it would mean boiling all water before drinking it and being frugally economical when using water for washing up and washing ourselves. In case these stringent measures were going to be necessary, I kept a couple of spare wash boilers filled with water so that we should at least have a good supply of drinking water in stock to start off with. We also stopped using the privy.

I hasten to explain. Our privy is a large, heavy-duty plastic bucket beneath the old wooden seat. Each time the bucket is emptied it is thoroughly washed out, the seat scrubbed, and the bucket (about one-sixth filled with clean water) is replaced. If we were going to have to fetch water from the stream a quarter mile distant then we wouldn't have any to spare for jobs like this. So we emptied the bucket, washed it out—and stopped using it. This presented no problems. When the occasion demanded we simply disappeared into the woodland, or whinchat plot, or wych-elm plot, or the grove of spruces, with toilet paper and a trowel. This daily search for a new quiet corner was, believe it or not, an interesting extension of our lives. There are worse ways of starting the day than squatting amidst soft needles in the cool, scented sweetness of a spruce plantation.

News was now coming to us of other springs in the locality which had dried up. Most farms around here now have a mains water supply and a spring drying up simply meant that water would have to be carried from the house to the animals in the fields. Land Rovers with milk churns of water in the back were now a common sight on the roads around here, and 'when on earth is it going to rain?' was the main theme of conversation in the village shop.

I remember the thistledown that summer. There seemed to be more thistles than usual growing on the hillside, and the light, hot summer air was filled with the blowing billows of down. They floated over the garden, tangled in the spruce branches, gathered in windless corners, and came bowling across the kitchen floor. Have you ever tried sweeping thistledown? It flies up over the head of the brush, and laughs around your ankles. Gather it up in a duster and shake it out of the door, and it comes giggling back through the window. Thistledown will play this game all day long, but I had other things to do—so the fluffy seedlings frolicked unchecked through the house, some of them hiding all winter, sitting saucily on undiscovered cobwebs.

The water from Minnie was no longer reaching the main pond. It trickled as far as the top two pools only, then dried up. The water level in the pond was now very low and the tadpoles were jostling for room. Once again 'Nature', in the form of a hungry blackbird, was stepping in to ease the problem. The blackbird simply stood on the bank and daintily picked out a tadpole from the water any time he happened to fancy one. We decided to try to relieve the situation. We disconnected the hose from the stirrup pump and laid it down the stream-bed. When we had collected the last bucket of water for the day we propped up the hose-pipe so that it caught the trickle from Minnie. The trickle ran down the hose-pipe, which by-passed all the little pools, and emptied into the pond. All night Minnie's trickle fed this pond and the tadpoles had a bit more room to move.

When I was next cycling to the village I decided to stop by the stream to explore a short stretch of the bank in order to seek out a suitable place from which water could be collected in buckets.

The stream is not obvious from the road at this point. It flows
through a narrow gully, and the road bridge arches high above
it. It would mean trespassing on land belonging to Mr. Jones
to get down to the river-bank, but I knew that he wouldn't
mind. I stopped at the bridge, got off my bike and leaned over
the parapet. What I saw made me gasp aloud. There was no
stream. The river-bed was dry.

Saturday, 28 August—Minnie's morning bucket: 1 hour
                                    3 minutes
                             Minnie's evening bucket: 1 hour
                                 $32\frac{1}{2}$ minutes
Sunday, 29 August —Minnie's morning bucket: 1 hour
                                 $9\frac{1}{2}$ minutes
                             Minnie's evening bucket: 1 hour
                                 40 minutes

On Monday, 30 August I went along the spring path with
my morning bucket and sent up a silent prayer to Araneida,
Sylvanus and any other nymph or deity who might be around
listening on that dewy summer's morning. I rounded the last
curve and confronted Minnie. I could see no water whatsoever
falling from her stony lips. I dropped to my knees, had a closer
look, and started to breathe again. There was water still flowing,
but it was so weak that it was doubling back on itself underneath the projecting ledge of stone and trickling down the
vertical rock face behind. I went back to the cottage, found an
old pillow slip and tore off a long strip of rag about one inch
wide. I laid this strip inside Minnie's rocky tunnel, and let
about three inches hang outside. From this three-inch strip of
rag came a steady drip of water.

Tuesday, 31 August—Minnie's morning bucket: 1 hour
                                 55 minutes

There was now no way of getting water down to the main
pond. Slowly the level dropped lower and lower. The blackbird
finished off the remaining tadpoles before the entire pond, including the deeper part, dried up completely.

Plants in the garden were starting to die. Several fancy
thymes were now dead. Some sage bushes and lavender were

suffering. The strawberry bed was burnt up and dead. All the leaves on the artichokes collapsed. The bed of artichokes stood like a forest of dead, bleached sticks, with the leaves hanging limply from the stalks.

One day when I was standing near Minnie I noticed a movement in the ground above and a bit to one side of the spring-head. As I watched and saw the earth moving I realized that a mole was working its way towards the spring. At first I watched with mild interest, the way one does when a wild creature is going about its business close at hand, and then a nasty thought occurred to me. The mole was working *towards* the springhead. At the moment he was pretty near the surface, but suppose he started to go down? And suppose he broke through underground into the spring passageway? And supposing the feeble flow of water now dripping off the end of my rag decided that it was easier just to slip away down this mole hole? With the instincts of survival taking over I moved quickly but carefully across the ground. I could tell by the rhythmic movements that the mole was right there, working just below the surface. Putting all my force behind it, I jumped upon the spot. Stamp, stamp, stamp! Don't you take our water! Stamp, stamp, stamp! I scrabbled down into the soil with my fingers and pulled him out. He was smooth, furry, warm and quite dead. Probably the first jump did it. I reburied him hastily. Alan came round the corner looking puzzled. 'What's happened?' 'Why? . . . Why do you ask?' I replied guiltily. 'Didn't you notice?' he said. 'One moment the birds were singing, and then they all suddenly stopped. Listen. It's all quiet.' I listened. There was no sound from our woodland; nothing but silence from the brooding conifers. There was a shocked stillness everywhere. 'I killed a mole,' I said.

Saturday, 4 September—Minnie's morning bucket: 1 hour 59 minutes

We still couldn't believe that she was going to dry up. Everyone else's spring had dried up, and so had the stream. The fact that Minnie was still dribbling *proved* that she was magical. Didn't it? For hundreds of years the Hafod cottagers had been taking water from this spring. We wondered what they would have done in the old days if the spring had dried up, and came to the conclusion that they would have gathered their animals about them and would have set off down to the Conwy valley to live alongside it until the rains came. But we couldn't do that. Apart from anything else, the Conwy valley was now part of the North Wales sewerage system. People weren't supposed to be taking their water supplies from the earth now; they were supposed to be taking it from taps in their houses. Now, in this time of drought, provided they didn't pull their flushes too often, nor draw water from their taps too often, The System would look after them. But we had chosen to live outside of The System. So far we had lived quite happily without The System's electricity, drains and water supplies. Were we now going to suffer for our independence?

Fire. It started in the Forestry Commission plantations above Betws-y-Coed, and swept in a powerful and uncontrollable wave along the Conwy valley. Although it was several miles away from us, and separated from us by the river Conwy, we could hear the roar of flames. The smell of the burning woodlands was terrifying. As night fell, so we could see the great fiery red glow in the sky between us and the mountains.

We gathered from the radio news that there were desperate situations like this all over the country. We began to think that this was the end of the world. This was *it*. It had come. There would be no more rain. The crops would all die; but it didn't make any difference, because fire would cover the earth.

We felt so vulnerable. We were surrounded by miles and miles of crackling, dry bracken and gorse-covered heathland. There were no pools or streams anywhere near us. There was no telephone at hand. One day, when coming across the common, we passed a family party picnicking at the roadside and were horrified to see the man of the party pouring methylated spirits into a little open stove. Alan dashed across the grass and kicked the stove over in front of the staggered face of the man who was about to apply a match. Fairly dancing with rage Alan pointed out the crass stupidity of such an action. His wrath must have been impressive, for the man apologized.

Sunday, 12 September—Minnie's morning bucket: 2 hours 2 minutes

A large beech tree fell across the Llanrwst road. No apparent cause. Mr. Jones of the village shop said it was due to 'tired wood'.

Then it rained! One afternoon the sky began to cloud over; a cool wind suddenly sprang up, there was a rumble of thunder over the mountains and it rained! It rained! Great fat drops the size of penny pieces splattered all over the paths and roofs. It rained! For about fifteen minutes. Then the roofs and paths began to steam as the sun blazed through once again, and within an hour there was no sign of moisture anywhere.

Wednesday, 15 September—Minnie's morning bucket: 2 hours 5 minutes

We lived in fear of what Dic and Dilwen might do. This was normally the time of year when they followed the old peasant custom of 'firing the heath'. Surely they wouldn't! Would they? We were given to understand that bracken and gorse were burned each year to 'encourage the growth of grass for the sheep to eat'. But we had seen the sheep quite contentedly munching gorse and pushing between the fronds of bracken to find the grass growing beneath. After a session of burning, there was nothing for the sheep to eat at all on that piece of ground until the gorse showed signs of recovery a couple of years later. Dic and Dilwen were well aware that the sheep fed happily on gorse because they in fact possessed an old gorse mill that their grandfather had used. Gorse which has been chopped can be stored for use as a winter food. In spite of this knowledge Dic and Dilwen burned parts of the moor each year. It was the custom. We guessed that we would smell the moor burning before we saw or heard it, so we were constantly sniffing the air, like a pair of worried dogs.

We felt a change in the weather. A slight wind began to blow from the south-west, and clouds formed over the mountains. It became cooler. The clouds gathered more and more each day and the skies were turning from blue to grey. Then the rain started to fall. Nothing very spectacular. A short shower one day; then a little more rain the next. But the weather had changed; we felt it. More rain fell, and a great, moist sigh of relief passed over the garden.

Monday, 20 September   —Minnie's morning bucket:
                                    1 hour 37 minutes
Tuesday, 21 September   —Minnie's morning bucket:
                                    1 hour 2 minutes
Wednesday, 22 September—Minnie's morning bucket:
                                    46 minutes!

Recovery was rapid. Minnie was now soaking up all the rain she could get. Water was trickling down the dried-up spring-bed and flowing into the main pond.

The crisis was over. Minnie had not let us down.

In the autumn we counted the cost of the drought. We had lost our strawberry bed, most of our fancy thymes, quite a few sage and lavender bushes, most of the pond mints, whole patches of stonecrop and saxifrage, and the little rowan that had been growing out of the old elder tree. But there had been no losses in the vegetable garden. The artichokes produced food for us in spite of the fact that their tops had died off, and most other vegetables gave us normal yields. The exceptions were the garden mints—all of which seemed to flourish in the drought (the round-leaved wild mint produced leaves measuring 5 inches by 3 inches)—and the seakale beet that gave us monster leaves, some of them measuring 18 inches by 12 inches. The parsnip crop that following winter was the best we have ever had. In the search for water the roots had travelled down and down. Some of them snapped off at two feet when we tried to lift them.

So it wasn't the end of the world after all.

14. Home economics

Come into the kitchen. This is where we spend most of our time, when we're not in the garden. The kitchen is the hub of the house. The front door opens straight into it, and the doors to all other rooms lead from it. Come and stand with your back to the stove and you can see the layout of the whole house. In front of you is the entrance to the parlour. Just to the right is the wash-up 'cubby hole'. In the left-hand corner of the room the stairs lead up to a tiny landing, a walk-in cupboard and two and a half bedrooms. On the right-hand wall there is a door leading to the back kitchen, which in turn takes you to the back door.

The kitchen is the living room, the workshop, and the main food storeroom. It is also the place you frequently pass through on the way from one part of the garden to another. During summer the kitchen door stands open most of the day. The birds, who have no respect at all for *our* territory, come in and make themselves at home. They hop across the floor to see what crumbs we have dropped from the table, or they come to seek us out to cadge a peanut. Sometimes they just come and sit on the doormat. Leaves, petals and seeds float through the open doorway and the scents and sounds of a summer moorland fill the room.

The kitchen is cluttered with *things*. Herbs, onions, shallots and garlic will hang from the ceiling hooks and banisters, in their appropriate seasons. The window-sill will contain sprouting potatoes, drying seeds, or germinating marrow plants. Alan's tools will be lying around certain areas of the floor, together with several current jobs that he's working on (such as a piece of wood to be planed down for a shelf; a pair of shoes to be repaired; a Calor gas stove for overhaul).

If it is washday, my boiler will stand in the kitchen; if it is the season of jam-making, the $\frac{1}{2}$-gallon Primus stove will be there. (I find it much more convenient to finish off jam on the Primus stove. The solid fuel Wellstood cooker is fine for the slow, steady cooking part, but when I want to suddenly arrange a good, fast, rolling boil it is much easier to plonk my preserving pan on to the Primus. This means squatting or kneeling on the floor whilst stirring, but I find that I am quite at home in these primitive cooking attitudes.)

The kitchen usually presents an untidy, muddled, but interesting picture. There can be no other kitchen like it. Few other women would tolerate it, but I wouldn't have it any different. I prefer, however, to have advance notice of visitors.

One day we were both busy in the kitchen when a man from the insurance company called. Our insurance policy made mention of cover for a television aerial. We have no television aerial, but we do have a windcharger. Could we have insurance cover for that instead? We wrote and asked the company. They didn't know what a windcharger was, so sent their representative to come and have a look. He arrived one summer's morning when I was busy making jam, and Alan was sitting in his chair beside the stove, his hands inside his photographic 'changing bag', loading a film into the developing tank. The roar of my Primus drowned any sound of approaching footsteps, and I didn't know we had a visitor until he was there, standing in the kitchen doorway, clutching his briefcase and looking in amazement at the scene within. Neither Alan nor I could leave our jobs to attend to him. My jam was just coming up to setting point and Alan was thrashing about inside the changing bag with a film that had somehow got jammed half in and half out of the tank. 'Go and have a look,' I shouted to the man from my kneeling position behind the bubbling jam. 'If you go around the house and up through the long grass you can see the windcharger on the hill. . . . Oh, just a minute!' I suddenly remembered that the last time a clumsy visitor had plunged through the long grass behind the house a few small creatures had been squashed flat, and I knew what creatures would be there today, sunning themselves all over the path.

'Mind the lizards!' I cautioned him darkly. The startled man left the kitchen. It was then that I remembered the other things I should have warned him about—the 2-foot-deep trenches Alan had dug at intervals across the path in preparation for the laying of drainage pipes; also the four bicycle chains, newly cleaned and oiled, that were hanging from a wire line across the same path. Within a few minutes he was back. I don't know whether he had found the windcharger, but I could see from the oil on his hat and the mud on his knees that he had found the trenches and bicycle chains. Rescuing his briefcase from where he had left it on the kitchen window-sill, the unhappy insurance man made off down the garden path, pursued by four or five demanding blue tits who were hoping that he was going to produce some peanuts. Alan, now disentangling himself from the changing bag, gazed after him curiously. 'What a peculiar fellow,' he said.

Needless to say, most of the work that is carried on in the kitchen has some connection with food. Bottling fruit, making jam and chutney is principally my affair, but we are both concerned with all other aspects of food storing and preparation, whether it is picking over the potatoes; stringing up onions; shelling peas for winter stores; or cleaning the vegetables for today's dinner, and making the bread.

We have been making our bread now for about seventeen years, and it has become as much a part of our routine as doing the washing-up, except that we need to bake bread only about three times in fourteen days. There is a lot of nonsense talked about the difficulties of baking bread. Don't be put off by warnings of critical temperatures, or long processes of 'rising' and 'proving', or having to use special 'strong' flour. If you want to get your teeth into something worth eating, have a go. Here's a recipe for you:

BARA HAFOD
Put into a jug: 4 rounded teaspoonfuls of dried yeast
3 rounded teaspoonfuls of sugar
about $\frac{1}{4}$ pint of lukewarm water

Give it a stir around, cover with a cloth, and put to one side. Whilst you are waiting for the yeast to get working, weigh up 2 lb of flour—either wholemeal or plain white, or a mixture. (I usually mix $1\frac{1}{2}$ lb of wholemeal with $\frac{1}{2}$ lb white.) Put this into a mixing bowl. Sprinkle into flour a teaspoonful of salt. Mix well. Grease and flour two 1-lb bread tins.

Now go and look at your yeast in the jug. It should be at least a quarter way up the jug, frothing and bubbling. If it's not, then it's probably due to the yeast being stale—not necessarily your fault, I have found stale yeast in a newly opened tin— so give it a bit longer. In fact, go and do something else for ten minutes. If it is still the same when you come back, never mind. Carry on and use it. It just means that your bread won't rise quite so well.

Make up the contents of the jug to about one pint with lukewarm water, and pour this into your flour. Using the right hand only (it's just as well to keep one hand clean) work the mixture around, squeezing and kneading between your fingers. After a while it should be in one moist, pliable lump in the middle of your bowl, with no flour sticking to the sides. If it feels too dry, add some more lukewarm water. If, on the other hand, it is all sticky and wet, add some more flour. Divide the dough into two equal pieces and put into your tins. Put the tins to one side, cover with a cloth and leave for about an hour. The dough should rise to the top of the tins. (Leave it longer if necessary.) Put bread into a moderately hot oven for about 40 minutes. By this time you should be able to 'bounce' them out of their tins. (If they won't come out easily, slip a knife around their sides.) I then usually put the loaves back into the oven, upside down, in order to get them crisp all over.

Please note that none of these measurements is critical. I have written down what *I* do. Alan doesn't measure anything. He simply throws in what he thinks looks right. Don't take any notice of instructions to 'put it in a warm place' to rise. You are more likely to put it in *too* warm a place. The temperature of the room in which you are working is quite adequate. And don't be misled by all this talk of 'strong' flour. I have been trying to find out what 'strong' flour is. On one packet it says: 'Blankety Blank is a traditional strong plain flour. This means it is rich in protein, and carefully milled to give the bread you bake more body, a better texture, and a delicious taste.' My cookery book, on the other hand, says that 'strong or bread flour' absorbs a greater quantity of water and so gives a greater volume and lighter texture. Yet another definition of 'strong' flour was provided at a flour mill where Alan and I once worked. Here a certain amount of Canadian-grown wheat was always mixed with the home-grown wheat when wholemeal was being ground. This, we were told, made 'strong' flour, and it was essential to have this Canadian wheat in order to make proper bread. So how did they manage in the days before wheat imports, then? Anyway, we disproved this by grinding for ourselves a quantity of pure Shropshire wheat that had just been delivered. With this un-Canadian, un-strong wholemeal we baked the most delicious nutty loaves we have ever had. We consider that the *freshness* of the wheat was the most relevant factor here, not its nationality.

So I am still not clear what 'strong' flour is, and am beginning to wonder if it is tied up with some political chicanery that dates back to the old Corn Laws! I have been told that Canadian wheat contains more gluten than English wheat, which might mean that a puffier loaf is produced, but it has certainly got nothing to do with the baking of good, wholesome bread.

Alan and I are fond of fruity malt bread. I make this by keeping back about a quarter of my bread dough, flattening it out in the bowl, adding one very large and overflowing sticky dessertspoonful of malt extract, and a handful of sultanas and some candied peel. I mix this up—again using only my right hand—into a brown, very sticky and sloppy mess. This can be flopped out into the same bread tin in which you are baking the rest of the dough (separated from the plain dough by greaseproof paper or foil). When you remove the loaves from the tin at the end of 40 minutes cooking time, separate the two halves and put back in the oven again upside down. You will probably find that the malted half of the loaf will require longer cooking upside down than the other half.

Because we make all our bread, cake and biscuits, and grow all our fruit and vegetables, we can live very cheaply, which is just as well because with our haphazard methods of earning a living our income is very small. A few slices of wholemeal bread 'and something', and a plateful of vegetables 'and something', is the basis of our diet. The 'and something' is the part we buy, and it will always be the cheapest commodity available in the butcher's or fishmonger's shop or on the grocer's shelves.

Here are two weeks of typical Hafod menus—one week in summer and one in winter. I have assumed in each case that the week started off with a visit to Llanrwst—which is why I have chosen a Tuesday. (If we are going to Llanrwst it will always be on Fair Day, which is usually a Tuesday.) If we don't go to Llanrwst there will be no fresh meat or fish eaten in the following week unless a neighbour has bartered a joint of meat in exchange for Alan's services.

Typical summer menus

Tuesday
Breakfast: Bread and butter with marmalade, honey or Marmite (bread will be toasted if stale).
Lunch: Cheese, salad onions and/or chutney, with bread and butter; fruit cake.
Dinner: Fish and potato chips with peas; fresh raspberries and cream.

Wednesday
Breakfast: Same as Tuesday.
Lunch: Hard-boiled eggs, green salad, beetroot, with bread and butter; fruit cake.
Dinner: Stuffed breast of lamb, with mint sauce, peas, carrots and new potatoes; gooseberry pie and custard.

Thursday

Breakfast: Same as Tuesday.

Lunch: Scrambled eggs on buttered toast, with chives and parsley; fruit cake.

Dinner: Cold stuffed breast of lamb with rowanberry jelly, green salad, beetroot, raw carrots and potato chips; gooseberry pie and custard.

Friday

Breakfast: Same as Tuesday.

Lunch: Sardines and green salad with bread and butter; gingerbread.

Dinner: Lentil rolls with baked potatoes and seakale or spinach beet; fresh raspberries.

Saturday

Breakfast: Same as Tuesday.

Lunch: Fried egg and mushrooms on fried bread; gingerbread.

Dinner: Corned beef with garlic, green salad, beetroot and potato chips; fresh strawberries.

Sunday

Breakfast: Same as Tuesday.

Lunch: Hard-boiled eggs with green salad and bread and butter; gingerbread.

Dinner: Cheese sauce over baked potatoes, broad beans, carrots and onions; stewed gooseberries and custard.

Monday

Breakfast: Same as Tuesday.

Lunch: Cheese on bread and butter (toasted on both sides in frying pan) garnished with chives and parsley; fruit malt loaf and butter.

Dinner: Mixed herb omelette with peas and potato chips; rice pudding and stewed gooseberries.

Typical winter menus

Tuesday

Breakfast: Bread and butter with marmalade, honey or Marmite (bread will be toasted if stale) *or* oatmeal porridge with milk and sugar.

Lunch: Jerusalem artichoke soup, garnished with chives and parsley, with bread; chocolate cake.

Dinner: Pilchard fishcakes, with chives and parsley, and kale; raspberry jam roly poly and custard.

Wednesday

Breakfast: Same as Tuesday.

Lunch: Scrambled eggs with chives and parsley on buttered toast; chocolate cake.

Dinner: Casseroled shin, carrots, onions, parsnips, swede, turnips, peas, lentils, garlic and mixed herbs, with baked potatoes; blackberry suet pudding and custard.

Thursday

Breakfast: Same as Tuesday.

Lunch: Sardines on buttered toast, garnished with parsley; fruit cake.

Dinner: Shin stew (water and baked beans added to remains of yesterday's casserole, together with additional herbs) and dumplings; blackcurrant tart and custard.

Friday

Breakfast: Same as Tuesday.

Lunch: Hard-boiled eggs with green salad, beetroot and bread and butter.

Dinner: Lentil rolls, with kale and baked potatoes; gooseberries and custard.

Saturday
Breakfast: Same as Tuesday.
Lunch: Baked beans on buttered toast with chives and
            parsley; fruit cake.
Dinner: Cheese sauce over baked potatoes, onions, carrots
            and Brussels sprouts; rice pudding and blackberries.

Sunday
Breakfast: Same as Tuesday.
Lunch: Cheese, chutney and winter radish with bread and
            butter; fruit malt loaf and butter.
Dinner: Omelette and peas with potato and Jerusalem arti-
            choke chips; raspberry sponge trifle.

Monday
Breakfast: Same as Tuesday.
Lunch: Poached eggs on buttered toast; fruit malt loaf and
            butter.
Dinner: Baked cheese and potato pie with kale, carrots and
            parsnips; raspberries and custard.

The 'green salad' will contain a mixture of herbs, 'weeds' and
vegetable leaves in season, chopped up with shallots or some
other salad onion. I also use herbs liberally in lentil rolls,
omelettes and cheese sauces.

At breakfast time Alan likes a pot of freshly ground coffee;*
I normally prefer tea. We always have a cup of instant coffee
for elevenses, sometimes with two or three home-made biscuits.
In the afternoon we always have a pot of tea, and occasionally
a slice of cake or a biscuit with it. Mid-evening we have a cup
of coffee and sometimes, in winter, we have a mug of cocoa at
bedtime.

You may think our diet is monotonous and frugal. But we

---

* Alan insists upon two luxuries: freshly ground coffee for his breakfast,
and some tobacco for his pipe. We must never become so poor that we cannot
afford these!

find it adequate, and we enjoy our food. What's more, we have plenty of energy and we are never ill. We have had no influenza, colds or coughs in all the years we have been at Hafod. We can only put this down to the large amount of fresh vegetables and herbs we eat, because Dic, Dilwen and Gwen, for instance, live far away from any likely sources of infection yet frequently one or other of them is suffering with some form of respiratory disorder. They eat very few green vegetables; will eat their potatoes only boiled or roast; and regard all herbs with great suspicion. (Parsley is allowed for purposes of decoration only; it is always left at the side of the plate.) They all eat large quantities of fried fat bacon for breakfast; they will get through half a plateful of thickly sliced roast lamb, with roast potatoes at midday dinner (sometimes with some turnips, cabbage or tinned peas); and for afternoon tea they have many slices of shop white bread, shop jam and shop cake. At suppertime the frying-pan will come out again with slice after slice of fat bacon and fried bread for all.

Muriel is horrified by their diet, but we think that hers is no better. Certainly she will eat a few fresh vegetables, but most of her food comes in packets from the local health stores. She studies her diet very carefully, making sure that she consumes the right amounts of everything—according to her health magazines. She takes vitamin pills for her nerves, digestion and energy, and she takes garlic capsules to protect her from infection. Yet throughout the winter Muriel seems to have a permanent sniffle. 'Ah, yes,' she will explain, 'but it would have been *much worse* if I hadn't taken my pills.' She grows herbs in her garden, but rarely eats them; and she has flatly turned down our offers of genuine unencapsulated, unpacketed, unmucked-about-with garlic. There is one item, though, that Muriel never buys in her health store. Eggs. Muriel has bought her eggs from the local grocer ever since she discovered that the local health store was where Dic and Dilwen sold their 'free-range' eggs. Dic and Dilwen's hens roam 'freely' within the confines of two old motor car bodies and a wrecked mini-bus. Lined up along the backs of tattered seats, or perched upon a grimy steering wheel, they peer mournfully through the dirt-encrusted windows. The eggs produced by this unhappy band of birds are, of course, caked in manure. Not to worry though, Gwen puts them all in her washing-up bowl and gets cracking with masses of piping hot water, frothing with detergent. After a good scrub they look fine!

As we are never ill we have to spend no money on medicines or pills. But we do maintain a comprehensive first-aid outfit. It is well stocked with bandages, creams and lotions, but we find that the items most often used are adhesive plasters and T.C.P. antiseptic. Cuts, scratches and bruises are the sort of wounds Alan receives fairly often; I am more likely to burn myself through clumsiness when reaching into the oven. Johnson & Johnson used to produce an extremely effective burn cream, and when they stopped making it a few years ago I was most unhappy. How on earth would I treat future burns? When the inevitable happened one day, and I burned the back of my wrist whilst reaching into the oven, I decided to try an old remedy I had read about—honey. I went straight to the honey jar, scooped out some with my fingers and plastered it over the back of my wrist. It was extremely awkward trying to carry on working with a honey-plastered wrist, but I wound a piece of toilet paper around it, held on with a bit of Sellotape, and forgot about it. The pain of the burn gradually eased and, after about an hour, I removed the toilet paper. My wrist was pink and just a little tender to the touch, but unblistered. I applied a further faint smear of honey, and the burn gave me no more trouble. Since then I have gone to the honey pot after each burn, and I wouldn't buy Johnson & Johnson's burn cream now even if they started making it again.*

The only other 'home cure' I can offer is for nettle stings. For this remedy we must go out into the garden again. Dock leaves are the traditional plants to use for the relief of stings from nettles, but I have not found them of any benefit. One day when I received some painful stings upon my legs I grabbed a handful of leaves from some clumps of mixed mints growing

* Very minor dry burns need only cold water treatment.

nearby and rubbed them briskly over my skin. As the green juice squeezed out and spread around, so my leg became slowly numb, and I could no longer feel the sting. I grabbed another handful—mainly spearmint, but with peppermint and eau-de-Cologne mint as well—and carried on rubbing. Result? Complete relief . . . and no bubbly marks left either.

15. Bringing home the bacon

'I'm going across to Dic and Dilwen's,' said Alan, 'Gwen's spin-drier has packed in. Expect me back in five weeks' time.' This last sentence is a family joke, delivered each time Alan visits our friends' farm to do a job. Like all family jokes, it needs explanation.

Alan's odd-jobbing at various farms is an activity that has slowly grown. From time to time he has been pleased to carry out minor repairs at the farm of our neighbours Beryl and Evan Lloyd, in some small way hoping to repay their many kindnesses to us. As a result of these jobs, his reputation of being a general 'fixit' spread around the district, and before long other people were asking him to take on work—for which he was generally paid in kind (a hunk of meat, a few dozen eggs or some fencing posts being much more satisfying a reward than cash). The time inevitably came when Dic approached him with a request. It sounded a straightforward enough job. 'The headlamp, it is not working properly on my old tractor,' he said, 'I wondered if perhaps Mr. West would have a look at it?' Alan was pleased to oblige, and so he threw a few tools into his saddlebag and cycled across to the farm, expecting to be back in a couple of hours. In fact the job involved numerous visits spread over five weeks—Alan becoming more and more exasperated after each trip. After the third visit he came home, grabbed a notebook, and started a diary of events on the tractor lamp episode. 'This is unbelievable,' he said, 'It just has to be recorded!' I give below the unaltered extract from his notebook:

Visit to Dic and Dilwen's to attend to fault on tractor headlamp.

1. Arrive to find old tractor with faulty headlamp inaccessible because it is in old barn, with new tractor stuck in doorway,

2. New tractor won't start. No sign of Dic or Dilwen. Apparently gone out on 'urgent business'.

3. Dusk is falling. Gwen tells me mains electricity has failed. Produces torch. Torch battery fails. Decide to leave job and return next day.

(Sequence of events over next nine visits.)

4. Arrive to find Dic has failed to move new tractor.

5. Examine new tractor and find 9 electric leads broken. Repair leads and renew a fuse.

6. New tractor still won't start; flat battery.

7. Dic finds another battery. This battery also flat. No electrolyte. Fill battery with water.

8. Connect battery charger. Battery charger doesn't work.

9. Examine battery charger and find plug fuse blown.

10. Take charger to house. Find house socket main fuse blown. Also socket switch broken. Find socket upstairs that works.

11. Find both charger input and output fuses blown.

12. Find charger input lead broken, also input and output terminals corroded under the grime. Charger ammeter not working; ammeter rectifier almost burnt out ($\frac{1}{8}$ amp. charge—after repair). Dic says he will borrow another charger.

13. Borrowed charger doesn't work.

14. Examine borrowed charger. Find all 3 fuses blown and transformer burnt out.

(Dic buys new battery charger, and the battery is charged.)

15. New tractor still won't start.

16. Examine new tractor. Find fuel filter blocked; moreover, tractor has no fuel and no water. Further examination reveals bottom radiator hose broken.

17. Carry out repairs to new tractor.

18. New tractor moved and can now get into barn. Old tractor not to be seen. Found buried beneath machinery and junk. Move machinery and junk, and examine old tractor.

19. Find that 'faulty' headlamp is in fact hanging to tractor by its wires, there being no bracket. No reflector on headlamp.

20. Find floodlamp not working. Rear number plate lamp is smashed. Neither (combined) side and tail lamps working, and no red glasses in them. Side and tail lamp terminals, wires, screws and nuts missing. Give list to Dic who says he will obtain parts.

(Dic goes to Rhyl next day to buy necessary bits and pieces.)

21. New screws too big.

22. Screws changed next day, and various bits fitted with great difficulty.

23. Find horn wires are missing. Find also various clips and brackets are broken or missing and lamp switch is faulty.

24. Make some fittings. Dic obtains others. Carry out repairs over next four days.

25. Repaired electrics now broken again by Dic 'testing' them, i.e. tugging the leads until they broke.

26. Re-repair electrics.

27. Job finished. Prepare to leave. Ask what time is. No one's watch works; Gwen says both clocks in house also gone wrong.

28. Make immediate escape on bike.

Exchanging services for goods on a friendly barter system suits us admirably. In this way we have acquired materials for house repairs and fencing, also food and manure for the garden. As we have rights of turbary upon the common (and our solid fuel stove works perfectly efficiently on turf) we need very little money. But earning the small amount that we *do* need is a perpetual problem. There is no regular employment for either of us locally. Alan has applied to the local council, to the G.P.O. and to various small engineering factories for work, but there have never been any vacancies. The Council and G.P.O. put him on their 'waiting list'. He is still waiting. In thirteen years he has not heard from either of them. From time to time casual, temporary work has cropped up; we have worked at the local flour and woollen mills, and for a while I had an office job in Llanrwst—but none of these jobs has offered a permanent solution to our money problems. The two main sources of income in North Wales are farming and tourism. The farms very rarely employ outside labour, and we have neither the room nor the ability to make a financial success of farming at Hafod. What about tourism? Well, we cannot accommodate normal visitors at Hafod, but at one time we wondered if we could sell them anything. Alan is not only clever at repairing things, he can also make things. People on holiday want to buy handmade things by local 'craftsmen', why not from Alan? Bellows was the first idea. Having costed the wood, leather and brass, Alan tried his hand at turning a piece of brass upon a friend's metal lathe in order to make the nozzle. He thoroughly enjoyed turning the brass, and produced an attractive, highly decorative and functional nozzle. He then drew up plans—and discovered that inferior imitation bellows were selling in the local craft shop for something just over half the purchase price of the raw materials. Ah, but *his* bellows were going to be proper *working* bellows. When I pointed out to him that people who come to North Wales to buy bellows only want something 'arty-crafty' to hang beside the gas fire, or the electric fire, or even a real fire, and wouldn't dream of actually trying to *use* them . . . he lost interest. He wasn't going to make cheap rubbish for anyone. What about spinning-wheels then? There is a great revival of interest in spinning and weaving, with people actually using their equipment to make things. Once again Alan went into the cost of materials and found, as before, that imported spinning-wheels were selling locally at a price far less than he would have to pay for the raw materials he would need.

So, we faced up to the fact that if money couldn't be earned at Hafod, then we had to leave Hafod in order to earn some. But leaving Hafod to seek employment meant owning a motor vehicle—which meant having to earn more money than would have been necessary if we had stayed at home. It was a bit of a vicious circle.

Going into service was one idea that worked quite well. We advertised our services as a stand-in domestic team. Are you temporarily short of a chauffeur/valet/gardener/handyman/kitchen-maid/cook? Then why not employ us until you get fixed up? We found that quite a lot of people were glad to take up this invitation. Where possible we tried to work out a programme which enabled us to attend to essential jobs at Hafod in between periods of work away from home. Unfortunately it wasn't always easy to organize this. A request for our services might come, say, in mid-August, just when we are at our busiest with harvesting vegetables, bottling fruit and making jam. It would be much more convenient if we could work through the winter months, and have the rest of the year at home.

We then had the idea of finding temporary employment as shop assistants in town during the pre-Christmas rush. I wrote to a friend living in the Midlands and asked what she thought of the idea—bearing in mind the possible difficulty of finding somewhere to live whilst we were working in town. We had a reply from her within the week. Two large department stores in her city were currently advertising for temporary staff, and she had paid a week's rent on a bed-sitting room for us. It was within walking distance of the city centre—not a very choice area, but bed-sitting rooms were in short supply and she had to snap this one up immediately or lose it . . . and she hoped she'd done the right thing. She had. We tidied up things at Hafod, threw our bags into our old van, locked the front gate and set off for the City.

We went straight away to the largest departmental store asking for Christmas staff, and were immediately taken on. I was surprised at the ease of it all. Having been prepared to waffle away brightly in order to conceal my extremely limited experience as a shop assistant, I found that the only question asked was 'Do you suffer from bad feet or sore throats?' There was a queue of us waiting to go through the formalities of being taken on—all shapes and sizes we were; all colours and ages. But there was another queue shuffling through the personnel department too. I gathered that these people had been given the sack and were collecting their cards. The atmosphere was generally bright and cheerful. Obviously a case of easy-come, easy-go (as I was eventually to find out). We both had a cursory medical examination. Same question asked: 'Sore throats or bad feet?' Then an hour's instruction upon how to use a cash register, and that was it. We were in. I was allocated to 'Toys and Christmas goods'—ground floor; Alan had to report to 'Household'—basement.

We managed to wangle lunch breaks at the same time and we met in the staff canteen on the top floor. Time was precious. One of us bagged a table at which to have our sandwiches; the other queued up for two cups of tea. (We always eat mainly Hafod food, even when away from home. Bunches of herbs and parsley had accompanied us to the bed-sitting room, also sacks of vegetables.) Over our lunch we swapped experiences. Here is what happened to Alan. . . .

He was supposed to be selling washing machines and refrigerators—which was rather unfortunate. We have never owned either piece of equipment and Alan isn't the least bit interested in them. He observed that all the machines in his stock were poorly designed and badly constructed; many had parts missing, or loose and about to fall off; several were damaged; and he reckoned that none of them would stand up to much use. As the store claimed to have a tradition of looking after the customer's interests . . . ('The customer is the most important person here,' said the notice over the till.) . . . Alan did his best to uphold this tradition by strongly advising potential customers to go elsewhere, 'where the rubbish might be in slightly better condition than this lot'. In fact, not many potential customers managed to get hold of Alan. He found it easier to wander round pretending to be a customer himself, and keeping well away from people who looked as though they were seriously interested in buying anything. When it became apparent to the floor manager that sales of washing machines and refrigerators were practically at a standstill, Alan was moved to the carpet department. They were always short of staff here because no one liked working out the customers' problems . . . 'Our bedroom measures 16 feet 3 inches by 8 feet 4 inches with a 6 feet by 3 feet 2 inches window bay. How much of this 4-metre-wide carpet will I need to cover it? And I don't want any waste, mind.' Alan didn't mind doing these calculations but, once again, he was appalled at the quality of the goods he was selling, and felt obliged to point out the selvedges that were fraying, the faulty backing material that was sometimes in holes. 'Why not go and look around Thingum-mybobs,' he would urge, 'Their stuff can't be any worse than this, and it might be better.' When carpet sales began to drop Alan was transferred to electrical fittings department. Now here he was able to be of more use to the firm. The rest of the electrical fittings department staff were middle-aged ladies who were constantly needing help with their lamp-shade displays that wouldn't stay lit, their pretty flashing on-and-off lights that didn't, and their electric fires that failed to glow. When Alan was able to repair an item, he didn't mind selling it, and for the remaining weeks of his employment he stayed in the electrical fittings department and gave more or less satisfactory service. In fact there was one customer who went away very happy. He had wanted 80 yards of low-loss screened aerial feeder for his single side-band V.H.F. radio transmitter, and 50 yards of 7 by 0·076-inch cable to run his portable, low-voltage equipment. All told, Alan spent about two hours with this customer who eventually went away convinced that our departmental store was the most useful and helpful store in town. 'How much cable did he buy?' I asked. 'None,' said Alan, 'we don't sell anything suitable. I referred him to Whatsisnames.'

These moral problems of selling inferior or unsuitable goods didn't trouble me. If I was employed to sell rubbish, then I would sell it to the best of my ability. Presumably people came to this store because they wanted to buy rubbish and if they needed my help then I would give it. In fact the particular job allocated to me seemed, on the face of it, extremely simple, and quite undemanding. I was a 'demonstrator', which meant that I didn't have to handle cash—just persuade people to buy, and then refer them with their purchases to the cash desk. It was rather ironic that the particular goods that I was 'demonstrating' were plastic Christmas trees. Putting irony aside, and determined to get on with the job I was employed to do, I was faced with the problem of how to 'demonstrate' a plastic Christmas tree. You can put it up, and you can take it down, and you can put it up again. . . . All day?! I had a circular stand measuring about eight feet in diameter, around which I could walk. The rest of the time I just stood. All the varieties of trees were displayed on my stand, and the ones I sold were boxed up and hidden behind a curtain underneath my stand. In order to combat boredom and backache I was obviously going to have to work out a series of self-survival ruses. I applied myself to the decoration of my Christmas tree stand. None of your itty-bitty hotchpotch of colours and 'dingle dangles'; my stand was going to be dramatic and eye-catching. Each day there would be a different 'theme' carried out in a single colour. Today we would be cool and blue, with glass and 'silver' decorations and masses of blue and silver tinsel; tomorrow we would be pink and fluffy, with bobbles and tassels and pink and white ropes of tinsel knotted together. I hopped on and off my stand all day—replacing trinkets, rearranging branches—determined to get a bit of exercise and keep my mind occupied. I was also going to try and sell some of the damn things.

Unfortunately it was October when we started at this store, and the people coming through the doors each day were not thinking of Christmas. Their reactions when they saw me and my stand ranged from incredulity to downright hostility. I tried the humorous, matey I'm-really-on-your-side attitude . . . 'It comes earlier every year, doesn't it!' I would say with a bright smile to people who passed by. Some giggled and went by; some agreed, equally brightly, and went by; but most just ignored me—and went by. 'I wouldn't buy one of *these* things,' one woman said brusquely, sweeping past, 'I always buy a *real* tree.' In a flash I was back there. Back on that high, wild hillside, with the wind moving amongst the Norway spruces. The lapwings would be flocking now; they always did in the autumn. They would be wheeling and crying over the moorland, which would be scented now with that warm, blackberry-woodsmoke sort of autumn smell. The last of the curlews would have left. I wondered if the fieldfares had arrived. They were usually with us during the winter. We had left a couple of small marrows growing; I wondered if they would stand a chance of survival. If we had a mild autumn and no frost, they might last on the plants until December. . . . 'I got a flat of me own now,' the little woman was saying, tapping me on my arm, 'and I want a little tree. I'm going to have a good Christmas, all on me own; I'm going to get in a few bottles, switch on the telly, and to 'ell with everybody else. 'Cos I got me own flat from the council now.' 'Madam,' I said, back immediately to the here and now, 'I have just the tree for you.' I produced one of our 3-foot-6-inch models from behind the curtain, and shoved a few odd pieces of tinsel into the box along with the tree. 'And I hope you have a jolly good Christmas in your new flat.' My first customer! I was in business.

As October ran into November, and 'Jingle Bells' and 'Hark, the Herald Angels Sing' was relayed in loudspeakers to the passing public, so people started to come in for their plastic trees. I became quite proficient at persuading people to buy the more expensive 'heavy-duty' ones. 'See how they don't topple when I shake them,' I said, giving a slight poke to a tree that was well weighted down with parcels on the bottom branches. 'No chance of the dog rushing past and bringing it all down.'

But I soon ran foul of the floor manageress. I could never understand why she was so belligerent. It was obvious to me that all my colleagues in the 'Toys and Christmas Goods' were very hardworking girls and women, who took their jobs very seriously. But they were constantly being chivvied by this aggressive woman who seemed determined to cast gloom, fear and worry wherever she went. One day she swooped upon me. 'We shall have to do better than this, Mrs. West. Our tree sales are down on last year you know. You just aren't selling enough.' I was ready for her. Producing from my overall pocket a comprehensive break-down of all the tree sales I had made, I questioned her on last year's sales. Which types of tree were selling less? Had she comparative figures for this particular time last year? I had kept my list up to date as another ruse to combat boredom, but now it was serving another purpose. I had a shrewd idea that this woman hadn't the remotest idea what last year's sales were like at this particular time of the season; she was just doing one of her usual bullying walk-arounds. But she wasn't going to get away from me so easily. Were we perhaps not selling such good quality trees as last year, I suggested. If I could see last year's figures perhaps I could see what could be done about improving the sales of the particular types of trees that were not doing so well. She tried to take the sheet of figures from me as she started to move hastily away, but I held on to it. I followed her across the floor, still asking about comparative figures for last year. She broke into a semi-trot in order to get away from me. She didn't come near my stand again.

The customers started to come now for Christmas trees. There were straightforward, no-trouble ones, who selected their tree from the stand, and carried off a box from under the curtain without a quibble. There were the cautious ones, who insisted upon having their box undone to make sure it was all there. (Quite often it wasn't.) There were the drunks and lunatics who simply came into the store to get warm, and seemed to make a beeline for my stand; and there was the awkward Arab. 'I want that tree,' he said, pointing to my creation of all-gold upon a fluffy, white six-footer. 'Certainly, sir,' I said, diving underneath my curtain. 'No, no,' he insisted, he wanted *that* one. I tried in vain to tell him that we had equally luxurious white and fluffy trees in boxes. He was not impressed. He wanted *that* one. But it stood right in the middle of my stand; it was a Saturday afternoon; there just wasn't room to start dismantling the stand now. I suggested that perhaps the gentleman would like to come back at the end of the day and I would arrange to dismantle it and have it packed up ready for him. 'No, no!' He looked at me in exasperation. How could I be so stupid? He wanted *that* one, *now* . . . just as it was —with all the gold trimmings. I hadn't the remotest idea of the cost of all the gold bits and pieces on that tree; nor had he. If he wasn't worried, why should I be? I climbed up on to my stand, carefully lifted out the tree, and handed it down to him. Holding it aloft in front of him, dangling and jangling with trinkets and tinsel, he made his way slowly towards the cash desk. How on earth was he going to cope with the impatient throng there? I couldn't bear to stay and find out and— coward that I was—decided that it was time for my tea break.

The ladies in the cash desk were the most hardworking, least praised and most frequently grumbled at members of staff. There were always long queues at the desk and they were con-constantly under pressure to work faster. One pay-day I discovered to my amazement that I was paid several pounds a week more than they were—and some of them had been with the store for many years. I felt that this was extremely unjust, and the next time several of us were together having coffee break in the canteen I told them so. I urged them to do something about it. After all, just before Christmas when their services were most needed was surely the time to ask for more money. I invited them to stress the unfairness of their being paid less than a 'demonstrator' who had been with the store only a couple of months, and who had no responsibilities involving cash. My words took effect. Later that afternoon I saw a little knot of cash-desk ladies marching up towards the personnel department. I also saw the floor manageress gazing at me across the store with a look of pure hate. I knew it would be only a matter of time before she 'got' me.

We became caught up in those 'shortages' that afflicted the population that year. First of all it was coffee which disappeared from the supermarket shelves, then there was the bread strike. As we were still baking our own bread . . . (other bed-sitting-room tenants please note—you don't *have* to live in a cottage to enjoy the aroma of home-baked bread) . . . this didn't affect us immediately, but all too soon the wholemeal flour started vanishing and I found myself joining the other women in combing the shelves of our own grocery department before the store opened in the morning. Then sugar disappeared. This was the most dramatic shortage because it seemed to worry more people. Quite often the store's delivery of sugar was bought up by the staff before the customers were allowed in. This panic-buying was infectious. 'The sugar's in,' someone muttered to me as she darted past my stand on her way to the grocery department. 'The sugar's in!' went up the urgent whisper all across the floor. From all counters and cash-stands the women started to move, 'The sugar's in! The sugar's in!' It was hissed up and down the aisles, urgent, and exciting. I found myself halfway down the store and jostling for a place in the queue before it occurred to me that I didn't *want* any sugar.

It was about a week before Christmas that the floor manageress 'got' me. I was five minutes late in returning to my stand after the coffee break, and she was waiting for me. 'Travelling time,' I declared haughtily. 'Travelling time?!' She started to go red in the face. 'Yes,' I said, 'we only get twenty minutes coffee break. The canteen's on the top floor, and with the escalators packed with shoppers it sometimes takes six minutes to get up there, and another six minutes to get down again. That only leaves eight minutes to queue up for and drink our coffee. In future I shall take an extra ten minutes to allow for five minutes travelling time each way. What's more,' I declared, warming to my theme, and well aware that I was having my last confrontation, 'I shall suggest to all the other women that they take travelling time as well.'

I had only another half-hour upon my Christmas tree stand. I was sent for by the personnel department and given instant dismissal. But as I left the store I had the immense satisfaction of seeing the floor manageress at my stand busily wrapping up boxes and surrounded by impatient shoppers. Now that she had got rid of me she was landed with my job. It was unlikely that they could replace me at this eleventh hour, and she was going to have to cope with the last-minute surge of shoppers in the pre-Christmas rush. This meant she would have less time to harrass the other members of staff. All in all, I felt that I had won this last round.

Alan studied his contract of employment. The 'Instant Dismissal' clause worked both ways. At the end of the week he collected his wages, instantly dismissed himself, and asked for his cards.

We had saved enough money to enable us to live at Hafod for the next three months without worrying about money. The snows would be falling soon; no doubt the Carneddau were already shawled in white. Miles and miles away, far and beyond this frantic city, there was a cool, quiet place where the trees waited, and the birds waited, and the garden waited—for us.

We pointed the van in the direction of North Wales and headed for home.

16. Living in the hills . . . a postscript

I intended ending this book at the previous chapter—with the return to Hafod. Comings and goings have been a way of life for us for the past thirteen years. The goings may have been sad and worrying, but the comings-home have been full of joy. When we arrive home and stand at our locked front gate, we are always amazed at the apparent stillness. Hafod is sleeping; waiting for us to return. When we unlock the gate and walk up the path the birds will appear; usually a chaffinch first, and then the tits. We dump everything just inside the front door and immediately explore the garden, going first of all to the spring, and then to the vegetable garden. There is a light wind singing in the spruces; a buzzard cries overhead and a ewe calls from the hillside. Let's go in now and light the stove. We're home.

This would be a happy, joyous way to end a book.

But it wasn't like that when we last returned. When we turned off the main road and started to climb the little road that leads up to the moor and to Hafod, we were dumbfounded to be stopped by temporary traffic lights. Men were working. Gigantic machinery was shifting earth. The right-hand bank of the road was being torn away. The old wall was being removed; the new line of the road was stitched together with posts and strands of wire. A long-standing but deeply buried nightmare was being acted out in front of us. The bulldozers had arrived.

We had always known that they planned to widen the road. It was inevitable. Each year it has been noticeable that more and more people have been driving up the high and lonely road that passes Hafod. More and more people have been looking at their maps and realizing that by driving up on to the Hiraethog moors they can get to Colwyn Bay without becoming snarled up in traffic at Betws-y-Coed or Llanrwst. We lived in fear that one day the local council planning office would look at *their* maps too, and see a solution to some of their problems by diverting traffic past Hafod. We comforted ourselves with the thought that the road would need far too much money spent on it for such a diversion to be feasible.

In the thirteen years that we have been here we have watched 'civilization' creeping closer to us. For century after century time has stood still in these hills. In the farmhouses and cottages the daily domestic routine, and the traditions of farming were the same twenty years ago as they were a hundred years ago. When we first came to Hafod, no one locally had electricity or a mains water supply, and fetching water from the well and lighting the lamps at dusk was an everyday part of life. Hafod is now the only cottage independent of The System. And when electricity came to this area everything changed. Almost overnight the people of these hills leaped from the nineteenth century to the present day; from candles one night, to fluorescent tubes the next. One day Gwen was stirring a black pot hung by a chain over the fire, and the next day she was fiddling with the knobs of a gigantic electric stove, and puzzling over the timer and simmerstats. Tachwedd (November) used to be the 'month of the killing' when the pig was slaughtered, salted down, and hung from the beams of the ceiling. Ceilings are all boarded in now, and a deep-freeze cabinet thumps in the corner. Colour television sets flicker in remote farmhouses, and countless half-understood electrical gadgets clutter up kitchens and yards. When we first came here, only Welsh was spoken and understood by the children who were too young for school; now they are more familiar with the latest television jingles than they are with the old tongue. The coming of electricity, more than the coming of the English, has been responsible for the decline of the 'Welshness' in these hills.

And all the time the road was being 'improved'. The grass verges have been reduced, the surface broadened and the whole road has been resurfaced several times over the years. But we had our first real jolt a few years ago when we noticed that trees were being marked with white crosses alongside the road near Llanrwst. The council assured me, when I telephoned, that they were only planning to remove a 'nasty bend'. But the whole road is a series of very tight bends all the way up through the woods; what about all the other 'nasty bends'? I was told that no decision had been made about the rest of the road. Then a couple of years went by; the crosses faded on the trees and nothing was done . . . and we relaxed once more.

Then the coaches started trying to squeeze their way along the tiny road from Colwyn Bay that links with the road past Hafod. But there isn't room for coaches, people said. So did they ban the coaches? No. They widened the road, and they built a wide, surfaced 'viewing point' on the topmost point of the high road. This is only about two miles from Hafod—and the coaches have now started to squeeze past us, no doubt looking for another 'viewing point'. They creep cautiously past us, because Hafod is on a bend.

We look at Hafod with a planner's eye. What do we see? A small poor-quality cottage, a few shabby outbuildings, and a lot of trees. The cottage needn't be touched; but those out-buildings will have to go. If the hawthorn hedge and a wedge of trees were removed, then the road could be straightened out nicely.

But a couple of years went by, and nothing happened. So we pushed it to the back of our minds again . . . until we turned off the main road the other day and found that the bulldozers had arrived.

There is something else worrying us as well. Something that we have refused to face up to all the time we have been here, something I have persistently ignored in the writing of this book. We cannot go on for ever living on a hand-to-mouth basis. So far we have managed quite well, but we now feel that our time is running out. 'Odd-jobbing' is fine and carefree when you are in your twenties and thirties; but we are now at the forty/fifty stage, and we are living through bad economic times. Knocking upon employers' doors asking for odd jobs is no longer fun. What's more, during these last couple of years we have had to spend so much time away from home earning money that we have fallen behind with the necessary work at Hafod. We are not keeping up with inflation either, and we cannot afford new clothes. This doesn't matter whilst we are here, but I felt self-consciously shabby whilst working at the departmental store, and was glad that my overall covered my old-fashioned and much-darned skirt.

There is a tempting alternative. We could stay at home and live on social security. None of our neighbours and friends would think any the less of us if we did. Living on the dole is quite a normal and now-accepted way of life in these parts. Just think of it; we could stay at home, care for our garden, have total security, no financial worries and we could forget about the outside world. Why don't we? We have this uncomfortable feeling . . . it has something to do with the fact that we know we don't really belong here, and therefore have no rights here. Other people might still like us if we went on the 'dole', but would we like ourselves?

We have always lived in hope that something would 'turn up'. 'One day,' I daydreamed, 'one day, when we're settled, I shall have my goats and my chickens. Something is *bound* to turn up.' But nothing did. Except the bulldozers.

It was the bulldozers that helped us make the decision. The end of an era has arrived. We must leave Hafod.

At about this time, the paperback edition of my previous book* was reviewed on a television book programme. It was late on a Sunday evening, and we made a point of travelling across to a friend's house to watch it. But we came away mystified. Some of the comments, although largely flattering, made us wonder if any of the reviewers had actually read the book! Our life at Hafod was compared with the lives of two fictitious people in a humorous television serial. (Are fictitious television programmes now the criterion of life?) One of these days we must make a point of watching this programme to see where we went wrong! However, *writer* Edna Healey (wife of the then Chancellor of the Exchequer) had obviously read the

* *Hovel in the Hills*

book and had understood and enjoyed it. And if the rest of the panel were appalled by the amount of hard work involved in living the 'simple life', Winifred Foley certainly had no doubts; she felt that if everyone took on a piece of land and tamed it, then there would be less trouble in the world today!

We are surprised that few people who have read my book accept just how poor we are. I have received many kind and friendly letters from people who have enjoyed reading of our life at Hafod, and some of them suggested ways in which we might overcome our problems with the cottage. 'Why don't you . . .

. . . 'rebuild the walls with cavity insulation?' they said,

. . . 'excavate floors and re-lay with waterproof membrane and insulation and incorporate electrical heating under hard-wood blocks?'

. . . 'fit new double-glazed windows with electrical extractor fans?'

. . . 'install electrical night-storage heaters?'

. . . 're-roof with tiles and insulate roof space?'

We couldn't even afford to buy stamps for letters of reply!

What's more, they seem to have missed the point. Hafod is perfectly comfortable so far as we are concerned. We have never overcome the problem of condensation—but we consider this to be *unimportant*.

However, we now have to face up to the fact that in our thirteen years of living out-of-step with the rest of society we have fallen way behind financially. Whilst our friends in the city have been paying off their mortgages, bringing up families, and rising in their professions, we have been wasting time messing about with stones and trees and flowers—and getting poorer. We have no professions. We have forgotten how to make small-talk, and don't know how to 'handle' people. But we know how to fix a slate roof and divert flood-water; we can communicate with a few birds, and we can identify a humming-bird hawk-moth. These things we shall never forget.

We have gained other things. We have gained an instinctive awareness of life; we have gained self-knowledge, self-reliance

and we have proved our emotional self-sufficiency. We have no
complaints; no regrets. We have been privileged to spend
thirteen years of our life living in the wilderness. For a short
span of time we have cared for a small piece of land. Because of
us, it is now more beautiful than it was; because of us, more
plants, animals and birds are living there now; and because of
us, the land is more fertile. If our garden is to be destroyed,
then we must make another one, somewhere else. We have
learned a lot, but there is still more to learn. We are older now,
but not too old to start again.

But it won't all be destroyed. Something will remain. The
grove of larch and noble firs at the top of the field may stay and
grow to become a landmark. Some of the Sitka spruces and the
Scots pines behind the vegetable garden will provide shelter for
the birds for many winters yet. The solitary oak tree in the
field—will it be allowed to live? And the little bluebell wood—
surely that will remain?

In a hundred years' time, when the cottage is perhaps a ruin,
a lone walker coming across the moor may look down from the
hillside and see the Hafod woodland, quiet and secluded at the
base of the hill. If he pushes his way between the overgrown
rowan, birch and cypresses he will come across the spring,
flowing as sweetly as ever. Kneeling down to have a drink, he
will see the stones that Alan laid. He will notice the arrangement of rock and slab; he will see the special stone of calcite
placed behind the falling water to catch the sparkling droplets;
he will see the flat slab placed for my washing bucket; he will
see the tiny, delicate mosses and ferns that Alan's fingers placed
between the stones; he will see the stonecrop and saxifrage. He
will see all these things and he will know that in this wild and
lonely place, someone once made a garden.

'. . . I prayed for: a plot of land, not so very large, containing a garden; and near the homestead a spring of fresh water, and a bit of woodland to complete it.'

HORACE
65–8 BC

HOVEL IN THE HILLS

BY ELIZABETH WEST

This is the unsentimental, amusing and absorbing account of the 'simple life' as practised by Alan and Elizabeth West in their primitive cottage in rural Wales. The Wests – she is a typist, he an engineer – moved from Bristol to North Wales in 1965, determined to leave the rat race for good. But the daunting task of converting a semi-derelict farmhouse and turning the unproductive soil into a viable self-sufficient unit was to prove a full-time job. The author describes the very individual and resourceful ways she and her husband tackled the problems which faced them – from slating the roof, curing a smoking chimney and generating their own electricity, growing a wonderful variety of fruit, herbs and vegetables on impossible soil. With a preface by John Seymour, author of 'The Complete Book of Self-Sufficiency', 'Hovel in the Hills' is a heartwarming and salutary tale which will either leave you yearning for a chance to get away from it all or convince you that the comfortable security of the nine-to-five is not such a bad thing.

0 552 10907 X

KITCHEN IN THE HILLS

BY ELIZABETH WEST

This is a delightful and remarkable collection of recipes (some of which date back to a war-time childhood) and is based very much on the old adage of making the most of what you've got. The recipes and humorous stories with which they are interspersed are largely taken from the thirteen years in the life of Elizabeth and Alan West when they lived in their 'hovel' in Wales.

It is a marvellous, entertaining and warm-hearted collection that is far more than just a cookbook, and will enthrall all those who enjoy cooking, reading and browsing between meals.

0 552 12072 3

A SELECTED LIST OF AUTOBIOGRAPHIES AND BIOGRAPHIES AVAILABLE FROM CORGI BOOKS

THE PRICES SHOWN BELOW WERE CORRECT AT THE TIME OF GOING TO PRESS. HOWEVER TRANSWORLD PUBLISHERS RESERVE THE RIGHT TO SHOW NEW RETAIL PRICES ON COVERS WHICH MAY DIFFER FROM THOSE PREVIOUSLY ADVERTISED IN THE TEXT OR ELSEWHERE.

☐	12698 5	Transit Point Moscow	G. Amster & B. Asbell	£2.50
☐	12851 1	Childrens' Hospital	Peggy Anderson	£3.95
☐	09332 7	Go Ask Alice	Anonymous	£1.95
☐	99054 X	Borstal Boy	Brendan Behan	£3.95
☐	99065 5	The Past is Myself	Christabel Bielenberg	£2.95
☐	12712 4	Island of Barbed Wire	Connery Chappell	£2.50
☐	09373 4	Our Kate (Illus.)	Catherine Cookson	£2.50
☐	11772 2	'H' The Autobiography of a Child Prostitute and Heroin Addict	Christiane F.	£2.50
☐	12727 2	Men	Anna Ford	£2.95
☐	12501 6	Beyond the Highland Line	Richard Frere	£1.95
☐	13070 2	Born Lucky: An Autobiography	John Francome	£2.95
☐	12833 3	The House by the Dvina	Eugenie Fraser	£3.95
☐	99098 1	Autumn of Fury	Mohamed Heikal	£3.95
☐	99158 9	Brendan Behan	Ulick O'Connor	£2.95
☐	99143 0	Celtic Dawn	Ulick O'Connor	£4.95
☐	99247 X	The Ford of Heaven	Brian Power	£3.50
☐	12577 6	Place of Stones	Ruth Janette Ruck	£2.50
☐	13058 3	The Marilyn Conspiracy	Milo Speriglio	£2.50
☐	12589 X	And I Don't Want to Live This Life	Deborah Spungen	£3.50
☐	12072 3	Kitchen in the Hills	Elizabeth West	£1.50
☐	11707 2	Garden in the Hills	Elizabeth West	£1.75
☐	10907 X	Hovel in the Hills	Elizabeth West	£1.95
☐	99097 3	Catch a Fire – The Life of Bob Marley (Illus.)	Timothy White	£3.95

All these books are available at your bookshop or newsagent, or can be ordered direct from the publisher. Just tick the titles you want and fill in the form below.

TRANSWORLD READERS' SERVICE, 61–63 Uxbridge Road, Ealing, London, W5 5SA

Please send a cheque or postal order, not cash. All cheques and postal orders must be in £ sterling and made payable to Transworld Publishers Ltd.
Please allow cost of book(s) plus the following for postage and packing:

U.K./Republic of Ireland Customers:
Orders in excess of £5; no charge
Orders under £5; add 50p

Overseas Customers:
All orders; add £1.50

NAME (Block Letters) ....

ADDRESS ....

....